The
Struggle for Law

By DR. RUDOLPH VON JHERING
Professor of Law at the University of Göttingen

Translated from the Fifth German Edition

By JOHN J. LALOR
of the Chicago Bar

SECOND EDITION
With an Introduction by
ALBERT KOCOUREK
Professor of Jurisprudence in Northwestern University

THE LAWBOOK EXCHANGE, LTD.
Clark, New Jersey

ISBN 978-1-886363-25-0

Lawbook Exchange edition 1997, 2022

The quality of this reprint is equivalent to the quality of the original work.

THE LAWBOOK EXCHANGE, LTD.

33 Terminal Avenue
Clark, New Jersey 07066-1321

*Please see our website for a selection of our other publications
and fine facsimile reprints of classic works of legal history:*
www.lawbookexchange.com

Library of Congress Cataloging-in-Publication Data

Jhering, Rudolf von, 1818-1892.
   [Kampf um's Recht. English]
   The Struggle for law / by Rudolph Von Jhering ; translated
from the 5th German ed. by John J. Lalor ; with an introd. by
Albert Kocourek.
      p. cm.
   Originally published: 2nd ed. Chicago : Callaghan, 1915.
   Inclused bibliographical references.
   ISBN 1-886363-25-0 (alk. paper)
   1. Law-Philosophy. I. Title
K230.J5K313 1997
340'.1-dc21   97-6826
                                        CIP

Printed in the United States of America on acid-free paper

The
Struggle for Law

By Dr. Rudolph von Jhering
Professor of Law at the University of Göttingen

Translated from the Fifth German Edition
By JOHN J. LALOR
of the Chicago Bar

SECOND EDITION
With an Introduction by
ALBERT KOCOUREK
Professor of Jurisprudence in Northwestern University

CHICAGO
CALLAGHAN AND COMPANY
1915

To
George W. Smith
of the Bar of Chicago
this volume is
respectfully inscribed

Contents

Introduction

to the Translated Volume

By Albert Kocourek[1]

IT is the fortune of the generality of men to follow the beaten path, to use tools already designed, and to think in terms already fashioned. In such lives there is no room for cataclysms, or great events; there is no place there, either, for quarrel with the existing order, or for effort to alter the accepted course. Such lives constitute the cell matter of the social organism, reacting mechanically, or at least without fixed resistance, to the influences from without and within. Rarely, however, in the complicated web of history, a labyrinth of lines will cross each other at a common point to mark out persons

[1] Professor of Jurisprudence in Northwestern University.

of great fortune or misfortune. Such was the imagery adopted by an accomplished novelist to explain his fatalistic views; and if there be merit in this sprightly figure, we will have no difficulty in conceiving an interesting conjunction of favoring lines to explain the brilliant career of Rudolph von Jhering.

One does not read far into jurisprudence without encountering both his name and his influence. He was a builder of new roads, a maker of new tools, and a creator of ideas. He came upon the world's stage as the last great influence out of centuries of struggle beginning with the revival of the study of Roman law at Bologna, and the successive stages of Glossators and Commentators, "Mos Italicus" and "Mos Gallicus," the Practical School and Natural Law, and finally the Historical School, to compose the differences between Romanists and Germanists, and to prepare the way for the Civil Code.[1]

[1] For a full account of the development of German law, see "A General Survey of (etc.) Continental Legal History" ("Continental Legal History Series," Vol. i), Boston, 1912, p. 311 seq.

Introduction

Jhering, the son of a lawyer, was born at
Aurich on the shores of the North Sea, in
East Frisia, August 22, 1818. He studied
law at Heidelberg, and (after the established
custom of German students who wander
from one university to another) also at
Munich, Göttingen, and Berlin. He became
a "Privat-Docent" at Berlin in 1844 just
as Gustav Hugo, the founder of the Historical School which Jhering was later to
overthrow, laid down his labors in death.
He became ordinary professor at Basel 1845,
Rostock 1846, Kiel 1849, Giessen 1852,
Vienna 1868, and at Göttingen 1872, where
he remained until his death on September
7, 1892.[1]

If Jhering had not become the most renowned jurist of the second half of the last

[1] The following sketches treat the life, character, and works of
Jhering more completely than can be here attempted: *M. de Jonge*,
"Rud. von Jhering" (1888); *A. Merkel*, "Rud. von Jhering" (1893)
(translated as an appendix to *Jhering*, "Law as a Means to an End")
("Modern Legal Philosophy Series," Vol. v); *Eck*, "Zur Feier des
gedächtnisses von B. Windscheid und R. v. Jhering" (1893); *Munroe
Smith*, "Four German Jurists," Pol. Sc. Q., Vols. x, xi, xii. Refer-
ence may also be made to volume ii, in the "Continental Legal His-
tory Series," under the title "Great Jurists of the World from
Papinian to von Jhering."

century, it is not unlikely that he would have gained fame in any other calling where personality, a comprehensive and lively domination of complex realities, or the literary quality might play a part in the attainment of success. The power of his personality is attested by the fact of his great popularity; his lectures were always crowded with listeners; and his home was the shrine at which the devoted from all quarters of the world worshiped. Ideas were obliterated and men effaced before him. Merkel, who himself became a jurist of great fame, says that after hearing Jhering lecture on Roman law, the discourse of Vangerow became a closed book. He was able to arouse great enthusiasm, to attract the multitude from within and without the university, and to enliven with bright colors the neutral themes of the law. He could sway the world both by his personal presence, and in no less degree by his writings. It is natural to speculate as to what might have been the career of such a man if his labors had dealt not alone with

the learned public, but with the unorganized
and unthinking masses in issues more stirring
than the unemotional materials of legal
science. At a hospitable juncture he might
have created or subverted a dynasty. The
literary quality of Jhering's writing is well
shown in the opening lines of his "Geist,"
which might be mistaken for the stately
measures of a sonorous epic. Another phase
is exhibited in the address here published.
Never before has a moral duty been asserted
with such eloquence; never before has a "lay
sermon addressed to the conscience" [1] been
more spontaneously and widely accepted.
Within two years this address went into
twelve editions, and although first published
in German more than forty years ago, it is
still being republished, the last German
edition being the eighteenth. At this time

[1] *Munroe Smith*, "Four German Jurists," Pol. Sc. Q., xi, 301.
Prof. Smith heard Jhering lecture on Roman law, and his able essay
therefore sounds an intimate note which adds to the value of his
analysis. This study also shows the dominating importance of
Jhering, and Prof. Smith's essay might well have been entitled
"Jhering and Three other German Jurists," for the others are only
as foils in the play.

it has appeared in nearly thirty different
languages, including Japanese. There have
been two translations into English, the present
rendering by Mr. Lalor first published by
Messrs. Callaghan & Co. in 1879, and a
version published at London in 1884 under
the title "Battle for Right." The present
work has even been the inspiration of a
novel by Karl Emil Franzos published (1882)
under the same German title.

The books of jurists do not usually come
within the mental range of the so-called
general reader; as a rule they are limited to
some definite system of law and to those
technically learned in that system. A large
part of Jhering's writings, however, carries
an interest uncircumscribed by geographical
boundaries, and has gained the widest reception of perhaps any European jurist, not
alone among those learned in the law, but
also among the cultured lay classes. It is
not difficult to understand this fortunate
and unusual extension of Jhering's fame; for
it appears to rest on two chief grounds:

first, that he treated by preference what Austin has called pervasive legal ideas — ideas of universal significance, ideas unlimited by the accidents of history, or the particularities of legal systems; and, second, that he had the faculty of powerful literary presentation. Jhering was a philosopher in the law, if not of the law, and had he been less, it is not unlikely that he would have remained a national factor of limited importance, instead of becoming an international figure.

Comparative biography was a completely realized art before comparative law was even thought of; and writers who have dealt with the lives of jurists have commonly resorted to the comparative method. In the case of Jhering the counter balance naturally has been either Windscheid (who died in the same year and within a few weeks of Jhering, and whose span of life was almost identical with his), or Savigny, the most conspicuous representative of the Historical School. The dissimilarities are striking in either case whether we consider the contrasted figures either from the point of view of personality, method, or ideas. Savigny, aside from being the leader of a great school, was the greatest Romanist of the first half of the nineteenth century. Jhering at the age of 24 had written a doctoral study, "De hereditate possidente" (Berlin, 1842), which already was considered a "remarkable dissertation," and when in 1852 (at the age of 34) he published the first volume of his "Geist," the star of Savigny's genius paled in the glare of Jhering's rising fame.

The theory of the Historical School, of an unconscious growth of law, was contradicted by Jhering, who insisted on conscious purpose as the dominant factor of legal evolution.[1]

Two observations may be permitted at this point: first, that fundamental theories in the science of law necessarily produce

---

1 *Tanon,* "L'Evolution du Droit et la Conscience Sociale" (3d ed., Paris, 1911), p. 44 seq. This part of Judge Tanon's essay has been translated as an appendix to *Jhering,* "Law as a Means," etc. (see note p. ix, supra); *Alessandro Levi,* "Contributi ad una Teoria filosofica dell' ordine giuridico," Sec. 34, p. 402 seq.

important consequences either first or last in any legal system. The legislative era could not have come to pass so long as the Historical School remained in the ascendancy. If it is to be supposed that Savigny intended to assert an irremediable lack of competence in the people to attain the conscious stage of legislation, then that distinguished jurist was spared some part of the mental anguish of witnessing the historical refutation of such a position, had his life been prolonged another quarter of a century. He himself became Prussian minister for the revision of legislation, and lived to see the formulation of the General German Bills of Exchange Code (1847) and the General German Commercial Code (1861) in the time of the "Bund"; but a benignant fate closed his eyes before the date of the imperial statute (1873) which authorized a commission to codify the whole domain of private law, resulting finally (1896) in the enactment of the German Civil Code.

The second observation is that any assertion of a simple unifying principle in the realm of causality is likely to assert too much. It is entirely clear to us now that there was an important element of truth in the theory of an unconscious development of law; it is equally apparent that the principle of purpose is also true. The error lies only in claiming an exclusive operation for either theory of law. It is, however, one of the most interesting phases of historical study to trace out the actions and reactions of ideas, and Jhering was a man who was able to do this with a lofty and inspired outlook on the manifold complication in the restless flow of life. The ascending spiral of evolution of juristic thought is plainly visible, to speak only of recent centuries, in the age of rationalism with its revolutionary by-product which gave way to an era of reactionary conservatism in the Historical School, and which later is supplanted by the epoch of legislation and socialization of the law. But, now, to attempt a simple generalization of causality in history, even with our better fortified knowledge, and in the light of an accumulation of experience, would likely be as dangerous and as inadequate as before. It should be noticed that when we speak of causality we enter the sphere of the historian and jurist, provinces where Jhering attained his surest fame. It is true that Jhering later attempted the treacherous problem of finality — a problem perilous even for the trained philosopher — but it is believed that if he had restricted himself to his earlier aspirations that his labors would have remained a standing monument of unquestioned juristic scholarship throughout the corroding processes of time.

Merkel makes an illuminating comparison between Savigny and Jhering sufficient in itself to explain the differences of character of these two great civilians.[1] Savigny, he says, retired to the shadows of his canvas. Both were masters of expression, but Savigny hid his personality behind his work, while Jhering projected himself in living reality in every line. He attempted, as Merkel again says, to

[1] Op. cit. (p. ix note 1, supra).

carry his reader by storm. Savigny sheltered himself in a mantle of reserve and directed his forces of ideas from a sequestered distance, while Jhering waged his battles on the firing line and determined the issues of war by the commanding aid of his conquering presence.

Of Windscheid, who was the great figure at Vienna when Jhering was the chief attraction at Göttingen, we may speak again in connection with a fundamental legal theory which has turned out to be of the greatest practical moment, and which has been a point of great controversy in German legal science for several decades.[1] Windscheid defined rights from the standpoint of protection of the will,[2] while Jhering made interests the essence of rights. The logical consequences of Windscheid's view is a formal, individualistic, and unhistorical conception of law; while Jhering's definition, on the

[1] *Gareis*, "Introduction to the Science of Law" ("Modern Legal Philosophy Series," i), p. 33.

[2] "Recht ist eine von der Rechtsordnung verliehene Willensmacht oder Willensherrschaft,"—*Windscheid*, "Lehrbuch des Pandektenrechts," 9th ed. (Kipp), 1906, erster Band, p. 156 (and note 3).

contrary, leads to the exact opposites, and invests the law with a positive social function.[1] Windscheid adhered to his position to the last, but Jhering's view has attracted the greater number of followers, and seems more nearly to indicate the real nature of rights as accepted by any of the present-day schools of legal philosophy.

Without the notion of interests, formulated by Jhering in the "Geist," he could not have reached the conception of the "Zweck." If rights are legally protected interests, it follows that the State must determine what interests it will select as fit for protection, and this question then logically develops the further inquiry of purpose in the law, which Jhering stated in the form of the principle, "the object is the creator of the law." On this three-rung ladder of reasoning, he attempted to ascend the philosophic heights, and whatever may be thought of his efforts it cannot be doubted that he laid a pragmatic,

[1] *Roscoe Pound*, "The Scope and Purpose of Sociological Jurisprudence," Harvard Law Rev., xxv, 2, 143; *Korkunov*, "Theory of Law" (Hasting's tr.) ("Modern Leg. Phil. Ser.," iv), p. 107 seq.

if not a metaphysical, foundation for a new juristic construction which enabled the law to emerge from the blind alley into which it had entered in following Kant.

It is perhaps still a question whether philosophies create movements in the outer world, or whether they only reflect or follow these movements; but in any case the social utilitarianism of Jhering came in season to synchronize with the most significant development of the law in modern times — the change from the individual to the social emphasis. Jhering's solution was not, however, the only escape from Kant's blind alley. The Neo-Kantians, too, have become social utilitarians, but their State yet has the negative character of a "Rechtsstaat." Stammler, the leading exponent of a revised Kantianism, is unable to lay down a single positive principle to govern the attitudes of the law. The difference between "do not" and "do" is all that separates the civilizations of the Orient and Occident, and a system of legal philosophy which makes the function of the State no different from that of a street-crossing policeman can never be productive of anything less unprogressive than a Chinese system of law. Even with its philosophic and psychological shallowness, the "Zweck" of Jhering is therefore to be preferred over the "Richtiges Recht" of Stammler.

Compared with an encyclopedic creator like Kohler, who many years ago engaged in a typically German exchange of ideas with Jhering in connection with the Shylock problem raised in this work,[1] but who has lived to supplant Jhering in the kingdom of fame and take unto himself the extraordinary distinction of the world's juristic leadership, the latter's works are not extensive beyond expectation either in bulk or item.

Briefly, Jhering's works are the following: (1) "Abhandlungen aus dem römischen Recht" (1844); (2) "Civilrechtsfälle ohne Entscheidungen" (1847); (3) "Geist des römischen Rechts auf den verschiedenen

1 *Kohler*, "Shakespeare vor dem Forum der Jurisprudenz," (Würzburg, 1883), and "Nachwort" (1884).

Stufen seiner Entwickelung" (4 vols., 1852–
65); (4) "Das Schuldmoment im römischen
Privatrecht" (1867); (5) "Über den Grund
des Besitzeschutzes" (1868); (6) "Die Jurisprudenz des täglichen Lebens" (1870); (7)
"Der Kampf ums Rechts" (1872) (the present
work); (8) "Der Zweck im Recht" (2 vols.,
1877–83); (9) "Vermischte Schriften juristischen Inhalts" (1879); (10) "Gesammelte
Aufsätze" (3 vols. 1881–86); (11) "Das
Trinkgeld" (1882); (12) "Scherz und Ernst in
der Jurisprudenz" (1885); (13) "Der Besitz-
wille: Zugleich eine Kritik der herrschenden
juristischen Methode" (1889); and posthu-
mously: (14) "Vorgeschichte der Indo-Euro-
päer" (1894); (15) "Entwickelungsgeschichte
des römischen Rechts: Einleitung" (1894).[1]

[1] Jhering has been fortunate above all his jurist contemporaries
in a wide and important extension of his writings into foreign tongues.
The "Geist" (No. (3)), and several of his other works have been
translated into French; there has also been an Italian translation of
the "Geist," and further translations based on the French, into
Portuguese, Spanish, and Japanese. Although no European jurist
is better known in America or England than Jhering, there has unfortunately been no English translation of this work, parts of which
are of great importance for what Austin calls "general," and what
Salmond styles "theoretical" jurisprudence.
  The "Jurisprudenz" (No. (6)) according to the author's preface

Introduction

Jhering labored diligently until the last,
and although more than seventy years of age
at his death, he left behind him many things
in preparation, unaccomplished. His impulse to create was boundless; each idea
developed a series of more general ideas, and
his physical body was unable to keep pace
with his mental activity. For this reason,
his chief works are admittedly only fragments.

to the eighth edition (1891) had been then already translated into
Italian, Hungarian, Greek, and (in abridged form) into Portuguese.
An English translation has been done by Henry Goudy (Oxford,
1904). This work is considerably used by teachers to good advantage; the present writer has found it useful in examinations in
analytical jurisprudence. Jhering's keen sense of legal realities is
here shown developed to the highest degree. No one but a man
thoroughly saturated with the feeling of the omnipresence of the law
and legal relations would think of raising the question whether a
guest at a hotel can take away the candles with which he has been
charged, or whether he can put into his pocket fruit served at the
dinner table (Goudy's translation, p. 24). Dr. Wigmore, dean of
Northwestern University School of Law, perhaps, under the sug-
gestion of this notable use of the incidents of everyday life, has
published in his casebook on torts a collection of instances very
similar in their novelty, interest, and analytical value.

The "Zweck" (No. (8)) has been translated into French and the
first volume is soon to be issued [now out] in an English translation of
Dr. Isaac Husik of the University of Pennsylvania ("Modern Legal
Philosophy Series," Vol. v), by The Boston Book Company. This
translated volume will contain valuable introductory material which
the present writer regrettably was not able to consult.

Legal humor is an ancient institution; it is the agency which
humanizes the bloodless operations of the legal machine. Even the
Olympian gods indulged their levities, and did not narrow themselves

The "Geist" remained uncompleted when he conceived the "Zweck," and the latter work was only a part of his plan to treat the whole domain of the normative divisions of social life. The present work was a fragment thrown off in the development of the "Zweck."

Of Jhering's achievement the "Geist" will no doubt be permanently regarded as his

to councils of lightnings and thunderbolts. Juristic humor, however, is something quite unknown in our literature. The nearest approach, to take a recent example, is Sir Frederick Pollock's "Genius of the Common Law," a work dealing with the strains and thrusts of our legal system. The chapter entitled "Surrebutter Castle" shows what a lighter touch may do with such a recondite and bitter subject as special pleading. But Sir Frederick's humor in comparison with von Jhering's is always somewhat Saturnine, or, even from another point of view, Euclidean. Jhering's contribution to this form of writing is his "Scherz und Ernst" (No. (12)) which is made up of anonymous articles published while he was at Giessen, and "Talks of a Civilian" published at Vienna. The vehicle is one of amiability, but the theme is a serious one for the law. It may be considered a loss to us that this work is not in English, since the problems raised there are just now of special interest in view of the widespread changes which are giving an entirely new character to the whole face of the Common Law.

Of the remaining works the "Vorgeschichte" (14) has also been translated into English. This work has not added anything to Jhering's fame, and it may be questioned whether he had sufficiently familiarized himself with the extensive range of working materials upon which such an ambitious undertaking should of necessity be founded. This work therefore in the field of universal history is defective for the same reason as the "Zweck" in the department of general philosophy, in that it attempted problems beyond the author's special knowledge and experience.

greatest effort.[1] When it began to be published, Rudorff, a civilian of the Historical School, referred to it in terms of reproach in his "History of Roman Law" (1857–59); but this reflection was one of the last feeble groans of an expiring and superseded theory of law. How frequently a fond parent is unable to judge impartially and justly of his own children is shown in the history of literature. Jhering rated his "Zweck" far above his "Geist," and could he have realized that the judgment of posterity would be otherwise, it would no doubt have been for him a matter of keen disappointment even though his preface to the "Zweck" foreshadows the result.

Jhering's creative period may be divided conveniently into two parts, taking his fiftieth year as the point of separation. The works of the earlier period are distinctly to be preferred against the labors of his later years. Although there seems to have been no abatement of his dynamic force in the growth of

---

[1] But cf. *Berolzheimer*, "The World's Legal Philosophies" (Mrs. Jastrow's tr.) ("Mod. Leg. Phil. Ser.," ii), p. 337 seq.

years, there is apparent a gradual declination in the sound value of their fruits. His posthumous writings are decidedly in contrast, and to their disadvantage, with the studies of his earlier years.[1] He rose up out of a national law to an universal law, but as his ideas became more general they also at the last became more tenuous. As a realist confining himself to facts which he apprehended with the intuition of genius, and dealing with "practica" he was incomparable; but when he attempted the flight into an alien country he left behind him the substantial products of a vigorous and fertile intellect to enter a domain as empty as the "Begriffshimmel" created by him for the Romanists.

Jhering's claim to great distinction may be said to rest, in summary, on the following grounds:

1. He universalized Roman law, approving at once its reception, and the changes which had been made in it in the middle ages, and thus took a middle ground which compromised

---

1 See. *Posener,* "Rechtslexikon," i, *s. v.* "Jhering."

in effect the rigid nationalism of the Historical School and the patriotic clamors of the Germanists. The Romanists would have imposed upon the country the Byzantine law, while the Germanists would have destroyed it root and branch. Jhering's attitude in this controversy is shown by the fact that jointly with Gerber, a Germanist, he founded (1856) a journal for the study of the dogmatic of modern Roman and German private law. This conflict between the law of a foreign and extinct empire and the living domestic customs was a heritage of centuries; and while the perpetual struggle had somewhat abated, credit is due to Jhering for throwing the weight of his influence in the direction of the only practical and possible solution of Germany's effort to attain a unified system of law.

2. He is the founder of modern legal realism, and the progenitor on the juristic side, as Comte is the ancestor on the philosophical side, of the Sociological School of Jurisprudence.

Jhering was a bitter (if not always consistent) enemy of the subjective; this appears

when he opposes, in his great work on possession, Savigny's animus theory;[1] in his conception of rights when he rejects the will
as the central factor; in legal method, when
he sets up a jurisprudence of facts against
a jurisprudence of concepts. The cultivation
of Roman law had developed into a deductive
process of legal reasoning which sought to
make the realities of later centuries and al-
tered circumstances of elapsed time fit arbitrarily the verbal form of ideas of the age
of Paulus.[2] But yet Jhering was not the
enemy of the subjective in his treatment of
legal evolution since this evolution itself is
the expression of purpose. Law is not only
teleological but psychological. The psychol-
ogy of legal institutions, however, must have
a factual basis, and can not be confined, he
insists, to a purely conceptual and unhistorical
system of ideas governed by fixed logical
constructions.

[1] *Munroe Smith*, op. cit.; *Salmond*, "Jurisprudence," 3d ed.,
p. 263 seq.; *Holland*, "Elements of Jurisprudence" (11th ed.), p. 196
seq.

[2] *Sternberg*, "Allgemeine Rechtslehre," erster Teil, p. 191 seq.

Introduction

It can hardly be claimed that Jhering was the first to raise the enduring problem of legal method, but never before or since has the purely conceptual method been assailed with greater vigor or efficacy. Jhering's chief merit here lies in his having brought this question into clear relief and in having advanced the teleological factor which resides in all legal rules. Neither the "Geist" nor the "Zweck" contains a minute and thoroughgoing analysis of the problem of legal logic, and the "Scherz" was much too literary in quality to furnish a solution. Jhering combated the over-extension of the conceptual process, but the ardor of satirical attack did not permit him to examine to find the boundaries of its necessary and justifiable operation. Nor does an inspection of the later literature of legal method disclose, in German literature at least, except in a few noteworthy instances, that the weapons of offense have been melted down to implements of husbandry.[1]

[1] See in this connection, *Gnaeus Flavius* (Kantorowicz), "Der Kampf um die Rechtswissenschaft" (1906), and the authorities entered on p. 50. The realistic trend of thought which had its

3. Lastly (passing over Jhering's unquestioned prominence as an historian of the
Roman law, his authority on various special
questions of dogmatic law, and his strictly
professorial labors), Jhering's great claim to
distinction is due, as already suggested, to
his treatment of the nature of legal rights by
which he established the juristic basis for a
social reconstruction of legal institutions.
His own interpretation of the test of legislative policy — social utility — may be re-
jected as amorphous, as a "mollusk of ideas,"
without derogating from the value and great
practical importance of his original discovery.
Unless it must be said that the world moves
on regardless of the thoughts of legal scientists
and legal philosophers, it is inconceivable
that civilized States could have broken the
barriers of the eighteenth century without

origin in Jhering's war on the concept jurisprudence is now known
in Germany under the name of "freie Rechtsfindung" after Ehrlich's
book of that title. Strangely enough, this tendency in legal method
has attracted representatives from the most diverse positions in
legal philosophy.

the lever of Jhering's idea. Little imagination is needed to portray a horrible distortion of social life under the pressure of learning and invention of the last hundred years, operating within the rigid mould of a "laissez faire" theory of law, government, and economics. On this count, and without reference to whatever else he achieved or conceived, Jhering is deservedly entitled to a leading place among the world's creative jurists.

Of the present work, it may perhaps with considerable justice still be said as was claimed by a competent reviewer on the appearance of the first edition of this translation,[1] that it is "the most brilliant, original, and significant book on the genesis and development of law since Montesquieu"; but it may be asserted with less provocation to challenge that it is one of the most famous specimens of juristic writing that the world has ever seen. The introducer may, however, be permitted to venture two brief comments:

[1] Albany Law Journal, xx, 444 (1879).

(1) a moral duty in the assertion of rights is an undemonstrable proposition;[1] and (2) irritation arising from an infringement of one's

[1] There need no ghost from the grave come to tell us that Jhering's proposition of a duty to maintain one's rights before the law has certain affinities with the doctrine that it is the right and the duty of States to make war. The same biological arguments support both points of view. Such militant programs to be thoroughly consistent must regard as undesirable all agencies which substitute for the wounds and destruction of the combat. In the struggle for rights, even the State itself, from this standpoint, must be considered a biological obstruction. Those who assert the moral right and necessity of nations to make war to serve their interests, do not hesitate to say that "law is the weakling's game." Jhering as a lawyer probably could not have accepted a principle so far-reaching and revolutionary, even at the risk of being inconsistent for his hesitation. Yet the only state of society wherein his ethical duty of self-assertion could be imagined to have any validity is one of political non-interference. In the primitive days of private vengeance such a theory probably would need no qualifications; but as soon as the State ceased to be a mere military machine, and found it expedient to interfere in private quarrels in the interests of peace, the biological argument became less clear and the moral aspect of the question more doubtful. For the ritualistic trial ceremonies of early law were not the same as the blood feud either biologically or ethically. At any rate, even though the litigant fought his own legal battles, and would not at that day, as a matter of honor, indulge the unmanly ease of a lawyer to speak for him, earthly and supernatural hazards had intervened which sometimes thwarted the bristling demands of courage. And now, in the modern age, when the State seeks to do justice between the parties, the hazards of litigation have become still more complex and fruitful. The modern court is little like the tribal assembly, and one now will hardly seek the law-courts to vindicate his courage or to promote his honor. A sad chapter could be written on the manner in which the State has discouraged the taste for litigation. We have only to think in this connection, among a number of things, of the

rights may sometimes be more effectively manifested than by procedural methods.[2]

ALBERT KOCOUREK

Northwestern University.

dishonored position of the witness which has become a factor of no little importance in making a resort to law unpopular, of the sensational press accounts, and of the machine patterned course of litigation. It is unlikely that any device except a simple reversion to primitive justice could bring out the spirit of self-assertion which has departed from the law and sought other channels of expression.

[2] Even commercial litigation is seeking an escape from the delays and difficulties of justice. It must be clear, therefore, that the procedural situation offers no advantages to purely ideal reactions against what the author calls subjective injustice. But there is a deeper reason which impels self-assertion to seek either the path of "club-law," or, more likely, silence. When Jhering composed this address (1872) he could hardly have foreseen the centralization of trade, industry, credit, and population which has within the last decades revolutionized the earth. In ancient society individual rights were submerged in the activities of the group. Personality has never been quite as well protected by the law as the claims of property; but when Jhering wrote, rights of individual persons had already reached their highest point in an evolution of many centuries. If anything can be predicted safely of the future one may, perhaps, say that the individual is again rapidly on the way to the loss of his identity. The modern world with its systems, its efficiencies, and its pragmatisms (and we say it with regret) is crushing down the picturesque freedom and initiative of the individual. It will require another era to restore him to the position to which Jhering would have exalted him.

Translator's Note

THE following extract is from the preface to the French translation of Dr. von Jhering's essay. The author, in the course of his work, refutes the Savigny-Puchta theory of the origin of the law. To explain that theory more fully, he furnished the following to the French translator:

"Scarcely was Germany free from the wars of Napoleon I, than the desire to see the laws of the nation reduced to a code was manifested, and Thibaut, one of the most renowned legists of the period, publicly employed his eloquence to promote that end. There was nothing surprising in the fact that this wish did not find the least favor among the princes and governments of Germany. They were only too well aware of the necessity in which their interest placed them to preserve, as far as possible, the existing confusion, both political and judicial, of the country. What was most to be wondered at, was that German lawyers who, it seems, should have had only one opinion on this subject, protested against this attempt, through the agency of one of their most illustrious representatives, Savigny, who, in support of this protest, published under the title: 'Vom Beruf unsrer Zeit für Gesetzgebung und Rechtswissenschaft,' (Berlin: 1814; 3d edition, 1840), a work not, indeed, very voluminous, but one of the most important in the history of German jurisprudence. Savigny's object was to represent as unreasonable the desire of reducing the laws to a code. Collections of that kind, Savigny said, were after all more of an evil than a good. They are not thought of in happy times, because they are not necessary. Rome is an example of this (as if the laws of the XII. Tables and the Prætorian Edicts never had existed), and in unhappy times (like those in which he lived), people possess neither the necessary political education nor the ability required for such an enterprise; and he endeavored to prove his assertion by isolated passages drawn from Prussian, Austrian and French legislation of that period.

"The irony of fate decreed that the coronation of his pupil and protector, William IV, should afford him the opportunity to exchange the professor's chair for the chief position in the Department of Justice, especially created for him. Savigny, the theorizer and opponent of legislation, had the weakness to accept the post, and he found the means to demonstrate fully what he called: 'the want of calling of our own time for legislation,' when the regulations relating to letters of exchange, and the German commercial code which appeared almost in the same epoch, strikingly disproved his assertion.

"The theory which he advanced on this occasion on customary law and legislation was not entirely new, but it is Savigny's merit to have presented it in its scientific light, and thus to have given it a claim to be called science. According to this theory, the earliest law has been, the world over, the law of custom. This law has neither been created nor sought for. It came into existence of itself, just as language came, and developed internally, in the convictions of the people, externally in the order of life. This law of custom is the natural form of all law, in the presence of which legislation is something artificial, mechanical, an encroachment into the order of nature. The legislator is, so to speak, to the law of custom what the physician is to nature. Nature should help itself; the physician should interfere as seldom as possible; for his very presence shows that the normal condition is disturbed and that disease exists.

"Thus Savigny entirely reverses the true relation established by the old teaching between legislation and the law of custom. With him, the law of custom comes first, and legislation afterwards. Why?— we ask in wonder. The author gives us no reason but his preconceived opinion, according to which such was the primitive condition of things. As the ancient institutions of the Romans

could not be traced to legislative acts, Savigny
concludes that they came into existence of
themselves. Might we not with equal reason,
maintain that the man who cannot tell who
his great-grandparents were, had none? Here
is the cause of this error. The memory of
the origin of legal principles is lost in the
course of centuries. That which, at first, it
was necessary to go in search of, to obtain by
struggling for, acquires by long use, a moral
authority over minds, so great, and an external fixedness such, that it seems quite natural
that it should have been always in force.
Such is the mirage which deceived Savigny.
His theory has no other basis, and it has been
possible only because the earliest time does
not tell us how the principles of law came into
existence. If, as became the representative
of the Historical School, Savigny had framed
his theory of the relation of legislation to
the law of custom in accordance with history
which affords certain information on this
question, he would have seen that the opinion
then admitted, and to which he attached so

little importance, was entirely true, that legislation is the normal source of law, and that the law of custom is simply a secondary and limited source of action. This opinion went too far only in the sense that it ascribed too much to the power of legislation. And, indeed, the omnipotence of the legislator was an article of the creed of the absolutism which governed in the seventeenth and eighteenth centuries. It was believed that all that was needed to change the very nature of things was a decree from high places, and jurisprudence itself shared this belief in the omnipotence of legislation. In this sense, Savigny's opposition to the admitted doctrine was most legitimate and beneficent, but this was not sufficient warrant to ignore the possibility and efficiency of a codification, and that great man in combatting an exaggerated doctrine fell into another and contrary exaggeration.

"His theory was developed and presented in detail in a work written in 1828, by Puchta, one of his most illustrious partisans."

That what Dr. von Jhering says of the origin of the law in general is true of the origin of the common law will scarcely be questioned; and we may therefore venture to say that this little work is likely to prove as instructive to the common law lawyer as to the student of Roman law. The "practico-ethical" question which it discusses is one not of times or places. It is as urgent in America as in Austria, and especially deserving of attention in the United States at the present time.

JOHN J. LALOR.

Author's Preface

to the Fifth Edition

IN the spring of 1872, I delivered, before a society of jurists in Vienna, a lecture which I published in the summer of the same year, materially enlarged, under the title: "The Struggle for Law." In its latter form, it was intended not for lawyers only, but for the general reading public. The object I had in view in writing and publishing the essay was, from the first, less a theoretical than a practico-ethical one. I was concerned, in preparing it, not so much with the promotion of the scientific study of the law as with the cultivation of the state of mind from which the law must ultimately derive its strength, viz.: the courageous and constant exercise of the feeling of right.

Two months after the appearance of the

first edition, a second became necessary; during the following year, a third, and the year
afterwards a fourth. When issuing the last,
my publisher proposed that I should prepare
a cheap popular edition, at a much lower
price, in order to give it as wide a circulation
as possible. This end could be attained only
by giving the work a much plainer dress and
by making the edition unusually large. As
even the previous editions had exceeded the
ordinary size, and as the foreign market for
the work grew smaller and smaller, by reason
of the numerous translations made of it, I
did not venture to believe that a fifth edition
would become necessary. But the fact that
a fifth edition is called for, is proof to me
that this little book owed its success, on its
first appearance, not to the charm of novelty,
but to the conviction of a very large circle of
people, that the fundamental view here advocated is correct; and in this belief I am
strengthened by the many translations of it
which have been made.

The following translations appeared in 1874:

1. A Hungarian, by G. Wenzel. Pesth.

2. A Russian, by an anonymous person, in a legal periodical published in Moscow.

3. A second Russian translation, by Wolkoff, in Moscow.

4. A Modern Greek translation, by M. A. Lappas. Athens.

5. A Dutch translation, by G. A. Van Hamel. Leyden.

6. A Roumanian, in a journal published in Bucharest.

7. A Servian, by Christic. Belgrade.

To these were added, in the year 1875, the following:

8. A French translation, by A. F. Meydieu. Vienna and Paris.

9. An Italian, by Raffaele Mariano.

10. A Danish, by C. G. Graebe. Copenhagen.

11. A Bohemian, anonymously. Brünn.

12. A Polish, by A. Matakiewiez. Lemberg.

13. A Croatian, by H. Hinkovic. Agram.

Author's Preface

In this present fifth edition I have changed the style of the work somewhat, and entirely omitted the former beginning of the work, for the reason that, considering the meagreness of my space, it had to do with ideas not fully intelligible to the laity nor of much use to lawyers. Whether it would not have been better, in view of the large circulation which my essay has found outside of the legal profession, to have omitted all those parts intended more for lawyers than for the laity, I cannot say. I have not done so, because the passages referred to do not seem to have at all interfered with the circulation of the work among the general public, and because, perhaps, the lawyer might not like to miss them here.

In the subject itself, I have not changed anything. I still consider the fundamental idea of the work so undoubtedly true and irrefutable that I look upon every word said in opposition to it as lost. The man who does not feel that when his rights are despised and trampled under foot, not only the object of

those rights, but his own person, is at stake;
the man who, placed in such a condition, does
not feel impelled to assert himself and his
rights, cannot be helped, and I have no interest in trying to convert him. Such a man is a
type which must simply be acknowledged to
be a fact. Egotism, without any redeeming
quality, and materialism are the traits which
distinguish him. He would not be the Sancho
Panza of the law if he did not see a Don
Quixote in every one who, in the assertion
of his rights, looked to any other interests
than the most grossly material. To him I
have nothing to say but these words of Kant,
with which I was not acquainted until after
the appearance of the last edition: "When a
man has made a worm of himself, he cannot
complain if he is trampled under foot."[1] In
another place Kant calls this "the casting of
one's rights under the feet of others, and the
violation of man's duty to himself." And
from "duty in relation to the dignity of

[1] *Kant*, "Metaphysiche Anfangsgründe der Tugendlehre." Aufl. 2.
Kreuznach: 1800. S. 133.

humanity in us," he draws the maxim: "Let not your rights be trampled under foot by others unpunished." This is the idea which I have developed further in this little work. It is engraven on the hearts of all vigorous individuals and nations, and has found expression in a thousand ways. The only merit I can claim is that I have more fully developed the idea. An interesting contribution to the subject of my essay has been furnished by Dr. A. Schmiedl, in his "The Struggle for Law in its Relation to Judaism and Early Christianity." Vienna: 1875. The saying of the Jewish professor: "Whether the object of thy right be a penny or a hundred dollars, let it be the same in thy eyes," agrees entirely with the position I maintain.

I now leave it to my essay itself to convince the reader of the correctness of the view which it defends; and in doing so I have a double request to make of those who feel called upon to refute me. I would ask them, first, not to distort my views and charge me with a desire to stir up strife, or with inculcating a love of litigiousness, when I only insist on the struggle for law where the attack on one's rights involves a slighting of the person also. The disposition which is ready to yield or to be reconciled, the meek and philanthropic spirit, the settlement of disputes, and even the surrender of one's rights are not always incompatible with my theory. What it is opposed to is simply the unworthy endurance of wrong through cowardice or indolence.

The second thing I ask is that the person who seriously desires to obtain a clear idea of my theory, would make the attempt, in the place of the positive formula of practical procedure which it develops, to put another positive formula. He will then soon discover whither his course will lead him. The question is: What should a man do when his rights are trampled under foot? The person who can give a tenable answer to the question, that is an answer compatible with the existence of law and order and with the dignity of personality has refuted me. The person who cannot do this, must agree with me or be satisfied with superficiality, the mark of muddled minds, which may indeed be rendered dissatisfied and landed in negation, but which can reach no positive view of their own. In purely scientific questions, one may limit himself to the simple refutation of error, even when one is not in a way to point out the positive truth; but in practical matters, where it is certain that one must act, and the question is only how he must act—it is not enough to disregard the positive directions given by another as wrong, but he must put something in their place. I shall wait and see whether this will happen in respect to the positive answer given by me.

One word more, on a point which has been contested even by those with whom I otherwise agree. I refer to my claim that injustice was done to Shylock.

I have not contended that the judge should have recognized Shylock's bond to be valid; but that, once he had recognized its validity he should not, subsequently, have invalidated it by base cunning. The judge had the choice of deciding the bond valid or invalid. He should have declared it to be the latter, but he declared it to be the former. Shakespeare represents the matter as if this decision was the only possible one; no one in Venice doubted the validity of the bond; Antonio's friends, Antonio himself, the court, all were agreed that the bond gave the Jew a legal right. And confiding in his right thus universally acknowledged, Shylock calls for the aid of the court, and the "wise Daniel," after he had vainly endeavored to induce the revenge-thirsty creditor to surrender his right, recognizes it. And now, after the judge's decision has been given, after all doubt as to the legal right of the Jew has been removed by the judge himself, and not a word can be said against it; after the whole assembly, the doge included, have accommodated themselves to the inevitable decree of the law — now that the victor, entirely sure of his case, intends to do what the judgment of the court authorized him to do, the same judge who had solemnly recognized his rights, renders those rights nugatory by an objection, a stratagem so contemptible that it is worthy of no serious attention. Is there any flesh without blood? The judge who accorded Shylock the right to cut a pound of flesh out of Antonio's body accorded him, at the same time, the right to Antonio's blood, without which flesh cannot be. Both are refused to the Jew. He must take the flesh without the blood, and cut out only an exact pound of flesh, no more and no less. Do I say too much when I assert that here the Jew is cheated out of his legal right? True it is done in the interest of humanity, but does chicanery cease to be chicanery because practised in the name of humanity?

RUDOLPH von JHERING.

Göttingen, Feb. 24, 1877.

The Struggle for Law

The Struggle for Law

CHAPTER I

ORIGIN OF THE LAW

THE end of the law is peace. The means to that end is war. So long as the law is compelled to hold itself in readiness to resist the attacks of wrong — and this it will be compelled to do until the end of time — it cannot dispense with war. The life of the law is a struggle,— a struggle of nations, of the state power, of classes, of individuals.

All the law in the world has been obtained by strife. Every principle of law which obtains had first to be wrung by force from those who denied it; and every legal right — the legal rights of a whole nation as well as those of individuals — supposes a continual readiness to assert it and defend it. The law is not mere theory, but living force. And hence it is that Justice which, in one hand, holds the scales, in which she weighs the right, carries in the other the sword with which she executes it. The sword without the scales is brute force, the scales without the sword is the impotence of law. The scales and the sword belong together, and the state of the law is perfect only where the power with which Justice carries the sword is equalled by the skill with which she holds the scales.

Law is an uninterrupted labor, and not of the state power only, but of the entire people. The entire life of the law, embraced in one glance, presents us with the same spectacle of restless striving and working of a whole nation, afforded by its activity in the domain of economic and intellectual production. Every individual placed in a position in which he is compelled to defend his legal rights, takes part in this work of the nation, and contributes his mite towards the realization of the idea of law on earth.

Doubtless, this duty is not incumbent on all to the same extent. Undisturbed by strife and without offense, the life of thousands of individuals passes away, within the limits imposed by the law to human action; and if we were to tell them: The law is a warfare, they would not understand us, for they know it only as a condition of peace and of order. And from the point of view of their own experience they are entirely right, just as is the rich heir into whose lap the fruit of the labor of others has fallen, without any toil to him, when he questions the principle: property is labor. The cause of the illusion of both is that the two sides of the ideas of property and of law may be subjectively separated from each other in such a manner that enjoyment and peace become the part of one, and labor and strife of the other. If we were to address ourselves to the latter, he would give us an entirely opposite answer. And, indeed, property, like the law, is a Janus-head with a double face. To some it turns only one side, to others only the other;

3

and hence the difference of the picture of it obtained by the two. This, in relation to the law, applies to whole generations as well as to single individuals. The life of one generation is war, of another peace; and nations, in consequence of this difference of subjective division, are subject to the same illusion precisely as individuals. A long period of peace, and, as a consequence thereof, faith in eternal peace, is richly enjoyed, until the first gun dispels the pleasant dream, and another generation takes the place of the one which had enjoyed peace without having had to toil for it, another generation which is forced to earn it again by the hard work of war. Thus in property and law do we find labor and enjoyment distributed. But the fact that they belong together does not suffer any prejudice in consequence. One person has been obliged to battle and to labor for another who enjoys and lives in peace. Peace without strife, and enjoyment without work, belong to the days of Paradise. History knows both only as the result of painful, uninterrupted effort.

4

That, to struggle, is, in the domain of law, what to labor, is, in that of economy, and, that, in what concerns its practical necessity as well as its moral value, that struggle is to be placed on an equal footing with labor in the case of property, is the idea which I propose to develop further below. I think that in so doing I shall be performing no work of supererogation, but, on the contrary, that I shall be making amends for a sin of omission which may rightly be laid at the door of our theory of law; and not simply at the door of our philosophy of law, but of our positive jurisprudence also. Our theory of law, it is only too easy to perceive, is busied much more with the scales than with the sword of Justice. The one-sidedness of the purely scientific standpoint from which it considers the law, looking at it not so much as it really is, as an idea of force, but as it is logically, a system of abstract legal principles, has, in my opinion, impressed on its whole way of viewing the law, a character not in harmony with the bitter reality. This I intend to prove.

The term *Recht* is, it is well known, used in our language in a twofold sense, — in an objective sense and in a subjective sense. Thus *Recht*, in the objective sense of the word, embraces all the principles of law enforced by the state; it is the legal ordering of life. But *Recht*, in the subjective sense of the word, is, so to speak, the precipitate of the abstract rule into the concrete legal right of the person. In both directions the law meets with opposition. In both directions it has to overcome that opposition; that is, it has to fight out or assert its existence through a struggle. As the real object of my consideration, I have selected the struggle in the second direction, but I must not omit to demonstrate that my assertion that to struggle is of the very essence of the law, in the former direction also, is correct.

In regard to the realization of the law, on the part of the state, this is not contested, and it, therefore, does not call for any further exposition. The maintenance of law and order by the state is nothing but a continual struggle against the lawlessness which violates them. But it is otherwise in regard to the origin of law, not only as to the origin of the most primitive of all law, at the beginning of history, but also the rejuvenescence of law which is taking place daily under our eyes, the doing away with existing institutions, the putting to one side of existing principles of law by new ones; in short, in regard to progress in the domain of the law. For here, to the view which I maintain, that the principles of jurisprudence are subject to the same law in their origin as in the rest of their history, there is, nevertheless, another theory opposed, one which is still, at least in our science of Roman law, universally admitted, and which I may briefly characterize after its two chief representatives as the Savigny-Puchta theory of the origin of the law. According to this theory, the formation of the body of principles of jurisprudence is effected by a process as unnoticed and as painless as is the formation or growth of language. The building up of the body of principles of

7

jurisprudence calls for no strife, no struggle. It is not even necessary, according to this theory, to go in search of them, for the principles of jurisprudence are nothing but the quiet working power of truth which, without any violent effort, slowly but surely makes its way; the power of conviction to which minds gradually open and to which they give expression by their acts: a new principle of jurisprudence comes into being with as little trouble as any rule of grammar. The principle of the old Roman law, that the creditor might sell his insolvent debtor as a slave in foreign parts, or that the owner of a thing might claim it from any one in whose possession he found it, would have been formed in ancient Rome, according to this view, scarcely in any other manner than that in which the grammatical rule that *cum* governs the ablative was formed.

This is the idea of the origin of the law which I myself had when I left the university, and under the influence of which I lived for a good many years. Has this idea any claim

8

to truth? It must be admitted that the law, like language, has an unintended, unconscious development, or, to call it by the traditional expression, an organic development from within outward. To this development, we owe all those principles of law which are gradually accumulated from the autonomous balancing of the accounts of the legal rights of men in their dealings with one another, as well as all those abstractions, consequences and rules deduced by science from existing laws, and presented by it to the consciousness. But the power of these two factors, the intercourse of man with man, and science, is a limited one. It can regulate the motion of the stream, within existing limits, and even hasten it; but it is not great enough to throw down the dikes which keep the current from taking a new direction. Legislation alone can do this; that is, the action of the state power intentionally directed to that end; and hence it is not mere chance, but a necessity, deeply rooted in the nature of the law, that all thorough reforms of the mode of procedure and of positive law may be traced back to legislation. True it is, that the influence of a change made by the legislative power in the existing law may possibly be limited entirely to the sphere of the abstract, without extending its effects down into the region of the concrete relations which have been formed on the basis of the law hitherto — to a new change in the machinery of law, a replacing of a worn out screw or roller by a more perfect one. But it very frequently happens that things are in such a condition that the change can be effected only at the expense of an exceedingly severe encroachment on existing rights and private interests. In the course of time, the interests of thousands of individuals, and of whole classes, have become bound up with the existing principles of law in such a manner that these cannot be done away with, without doing the greatest injury to the former. To question the principle of law or the institution, means a declaration of war against all these interests, the tearing away of a polyp which resists the effort with a thousand arms. Hence every such attempt, in natural obedience to the law of self-preservation, calls forth the most violent opposition of the imperiled interests, and with it a struggle in which, as in every struggle, the issue is decided not by the weight of reason, but by the relative strength of opposing forces; the result being not infrequently the same as in the parallelogram of forces — a deviation from the original line towards the diagonal. Only thus does it become intelligible, that institutions on which public opinion has long since passed sentence of death continue to enjoy life for a great length of time. It is not the *vis inertiæ* which preserves their life, but the power of resistance of the interests centering about their existence.

But in all such cases, wherever the existing law is backed by interests, the new has to undergo a struggle to force its way into the world — a struggle which not infrequently lasts over a whole century. This struggle reaches its highest degree of intensity when

the interests in question have assumed the
form of vested rights. Here we find two
parties opposed each to the other, each of
which takes as its device the sacredness of
the law; the one that of the historical law,
the law of the past; the other that of the law
which is ever coming into existence, ever
renewing its youth, the eternal, primordial
law of mankind. A case of conflict of the
idea of law with itself which, for the individuals who have staked all their strength and
their very being for their convictions and
finally succumb to the supreme decree of
history, has in it something that is really
tragic. All the great achievements which
the history of the law has to record — the
abolition of slavery, of serfdom, the freedom
of landed property, of industry, of conscience, etc.— all have had to be won, in
the first instance, in this manner, by the most
violent struggles, which often lasted for
centuries. Not infrequently streams of blood,
and everywhere rights trampled under foot,
mark the way which the law has traveled

during such conflict. For the law is Saturn devouring his own children. The law can renew its youth only by breaking with its own past. A concrete legal right or principle of law, which, simply because it has come into existence, claims an unlimited and therefore eternal existence, is a child lifting its arm against its own mother; it despises the idea of the law when it appeals to that idea; for the idea of the law is an eternal Becoming; but that which has Become must yield to the new Becoming, since

——— Alles was entsteht,
Ist werth dass es zu Grunde geht.

And thus the historical development of law presents us with a picture of research, struggle, fight, in short of toilsome, wearying endeavor. The human mind working unconsciously towards the formation of language is met by no forcible resistance, and art has no opponent to overcome but its own past — the prevailing taste. It is not so with law considered as an end. Cast into the chaotic whirl of human aims, endeavors, interests,

it has forever to feel and seek in order to find
the right way, and when it has found it, to
overthrow the obstacles which would impede
its course. If it be an undoubted fact, that
this development, like that of art or language,
is governed by law and is uniform, it cannot
be denied that it departs largely from the
latter in the manner in which it takes place;
and in this sense, therefore, we are compelled
decidedly to reject the parallel instituted by
Savigny — a parallel which found universal
favor so rapidly — between law on the one
hand and language and art on the other.
This doctrine is false, but not dangerous as
a philosophical opinion. As a political maxim, however, it contains an error pregnant
with the most ominous consequences imaginable, because it feeds man with hope where
he should act, and act with a full and clear
consciousness of the object aimed at, and
with all his strength. It feeds him with the
hope that things will take care of themselves,
and that the best he can do is to fold his
arms and confidently wait for what may

gradually spring to light from that primitive source of all law called: the natural conviction of legal right.   Hence the aversion of Savigny and of all his disciples to the interference of legislation, and hence the complete ignoring of the real meaning of custom, in the Puchta theory of the law of custom. Custom to Puchta is nothing but a mere mode of discovering the conviction as to what is legally right: but that this very conviction is first formed through the agency of its own action, that through this action it first demonstrates its power and its calling to govern life; in short that the principle: the law is an idea which involves force — to this the eyes of this great mind were entirely closed. But, in this, Puchta was only paying tribute to the time in which he lived. For his time was the romantic in our poetry, and the person who does not recoil from transferring the idea of the romantic to jurisprudence, and who will take the trouble to compare the corresponding directions followed in the two spheres with one another, will perhaps not

find fault with me when I allege that the
Historical School in law might just as well
have been called the romantic. That law
and the principles of legal right come into
existence or are formed painlessly, without
trouble, without action, like the vegetable
creation, is a really romantic notion, that is,
a notion based on a false idealization of past
conditions. Stern reality teaches us the contrary, and not alone that small part of that
reality which we have before our eyes ourselves, and which presents us, almost everywhere, with the most strenuous endeavors of
nations in respect to the formation of their
legal relations — questions of the gravest
nature which crowd one upon another; but
the impression remains the same, no matter
what part of the past we contemplate.
Savigny's theory can, therefore, appeal to
nothing but prehistoric times of which we
have no information. But if we may be
permitted to indulge in hypothesis in relation
to them, I am willing to oppose to Savigny's,
which represents them as the time of the

peaceable, gentle evolution of the principles
of law from the inner consciousness of popular
conviction, my own hypothesis, which is
diametrically opposed to his; and it will have
to be granted to me that, to say the least, it
has in its favor, the analogy of what we can
see of the historical development of law, and
as I believe, the advantage, likewise, of
greater psychological probability. Primitive
times! It was once the fashion to deck them
out in every beautiful quality: truth, frank-
ness, fidelity, simplicity, religious faith; and
in such soil, principles of law would certainly
have been able to thrive without any other
force to assist their growth than the power
of the conviction of right: they would not
have needed the sword, nor even the unassist-
ed arm. But to-day we all know that the
pious and hoary past was noted for qualities
the very opposite of these, and the supposition
that they were able to get their principles of
law in an easier manner than all later generations can scarcely expect to be credited now.
For my part, I am convinced that the labor

which they must have expended on their task, was one still more difficult, and that even the simplest principles of law, such for instance as those named above, from the most ancient Roman law, of the authority of the owner to claim back his chattel from any one in whose possession it was found, and of the creditor to sell his insolvent debtor into foreign servitude, had to be first fought out by the hardest battles, before they obtained unquestioned recognition. But be this as it may, we may leave the most primitive times out of consideration. The information afforded us by the remotest history on the origin of law is sufficient. But this information is to the effect: the birth of law like that of men has been uniformly attended by the violent throes of childbirth.

And why should we complain that it is thus attended? The very fact that their law does not fall to the lot of nations without trouble, that they have had to struggle, to battle and to bleed for it, creates between nations and their laws the same intimate bond as is created between the mother and her child when, at its birth, she stakes her own life. A principle of law won without toil is on a level with the children brought by the stork: what the stork has brought, the fox or the vulture can take away again. But from the mother who gave it birth, neither the fox nor the vulture can take the child away; and just as little can a people be deprived of the laws or institutions which they have had to labor and to bleed for, in order to obtain. We may even claim that the energy and love with which a people hold to and assert their laws, are determined by the amount of toil and effort which it cost them to obtain them. Not mere custom, but sacrifice, forges the strongest bond between a people and their principles of legal right; and God does not make a gift of what it needs to the nation He wishes well, nor does He make the labor necessary to its acquisition easy, but difficult. In this sense, I do not hesitate to say: The struggle needed by laws to fight their way into existence is not a curse, but a blessing.

CHAPTER II

THE LIFE OF THE LAW A STRUGGLE

NOW turn to the real subject of my essay — the struggle for concrete law. This struggle is provoked by the violation or the withholding of legal rights. Since no legal right, be it the right of an individual or of a nation, is guarded against this danger, it follows that this struggle may be repeated in every sphere of the law — in the valleys of private law, as well as on the heights of public and international law. War, sedition, revolution, so-called lynch-law, the club-law, and feudal law of the middle ages, and the last remnant of it in our own times, the duel; lastly, self-defense, and the action at law — what are they all, spite of the difference of the object striven for and of the thing which is staked, of the form and dimensions of the struggle — what but forms and scenes of the one same drama, the struggle for rights, the struggle for the principles of law? If now, of all these forms, I choose the least violent, the legal struggle for individual rights in the form of an action at law, it is not because it has for jurists a higher interest than any other, but because, in a trial at law, the real nature of the case is most subject to the danger of being ignored both by jurists and the laity. In all other instances this real nature of the case appears in all its clearness. That in all other instances there is question of wealth or goods which warrant and repay great risk, even the dullest mind understands, and no one will, in such instances, raise the question: Why fight; why not rather yield? The magnificence of the sight of the highest display of human strength and sacrifice irresistibly carries all of us along with it and lifts us to the height of ideal judgment. But, in the struggle for individual private rights, just mentioned, the case is very different. The relative smallness of the interests with which it is concerned — uniformly the question of mine and thine, the dull prosiness which uniformly attaches to this question — makes of this struggle, it would seem, simply a matter of cold calculation and sober contemplation; and the forms in which it moves (the mechanical routine of litigation, with the exclusion of all free, individual action and of the claimant himself) are ill calculated to weaken the unfavorable impression. However, even in the case of the action at law, there was a time when the parties to the action themselves were called on to enter the lists, and when the true meaning of the struggle was thus made to appear. While the sword still decided the controversy concerning mine and thine, when the medieval knight sent the challenge to his opponent, even the non-participant may have been forced to surmise that, in the struggle, there was question not only of the value of the thing, of averting a pecuniary loss, but that the person, in the thing, defended himself, his rights and his honor.

But we shall not need to conjure up a condition of things long past and vanished to discover from it the meaning of that which, even if different in form, is in essence the same to-day. A glance at the phenomena of our actual life and psychological self-observation will perform the same service for us.

Whenever a person's legal right is violated, he is placed face to face with the question, whether he will assert his right, resist his opponent — that is, engage in a struggle; or whether, in order to avoid this, he will leave right in the lurch. The decision of this question rests entirely with himself. Whatever his answer to the question may be, some sacrifice accompanies it in both cases. In the one case, the law is sacrificed to peace; in the other, peace is sacrificed to the law. Hence, the question seems to formulate itself thus: Which sacrifice, according to the individual circumstances of the case and of the person, is the more bearable? The rich man will, for the sake of peace, sacrifice the amount in controversy, which to him is insignificant; and the poor man, to whom this same amount is comparatively great, will sacrifice his peace for its sake. Thus would the question of the struggle for the principles of law reduce itself to a simple problem in arithmetic, in which advantage and disadvantage are weighed one against the other, by each side, and the decision thus reached.

But that this is really by no means the case, every one knows. Daily experience shows us cases at law in which the value of the object in controversy is out of all proportion to the prospective expenditure of trouble, excitement, and money. No one who has dropped a dollar into a stream will give two to get it back again. For him, indeed, the question, how much he will expend upon its recovery, is a simple problem in arithmetic. But why does he not go through the same process of calculation when he contemplates a suit at law? Do not say that he calculates on winning it, and that the costs of the suit will fall upon his opponent. Every lawyer knows that the sure prospect of having to pay dearly for victory does not keep many persons from suing. How frequently it happens that the counselor who exposes to a client the badness of his case and dissuades him from suing receives for answer: Bring suit, cost what it may!

How explain this mode of action which, from the standpoint of a rational estimation of material interests, is simply senseless?

The answer usually given to this question is well known. It is, we are told, the miserable mania for litigation, the pure love of wrangling, the irresistible desire to inflict pain on one's opponent, even when it is certain that one will have to pay for it more heavily than one's opponent.

Let us drop the consideration of the controversy between two private persons, and in their place put two nations. The one nation, let us suppose, has, contrary to law, taken from the other a square mile of barren, worthless land. Shall the latter go to war? Let us examine the question from precisely the same standpoint from which the theory of the mania for litigation judges it, in the case of the peasant from whose land a neighbor has

26

ploughed away a few feet, or into whose
meadow he has thrown a few stones. What
signifies a square mile of barren land compared with a war which costs the lives of
thousands, brings sorrow and misery into
the palace and the hut, eats up millions and
millions of the treasure of the state, and
possibly imperils its existence? What folly
to make such a sacrifice for such an end!

Such would have to be our judgment, if
the peasant and the nation were measured
with the same measure. Yet no one would
wish to give to the nation the same advice as
to the peasant. Every one feels that a nation
which looked upon such a violation of law in
silence would have signed its own death
sentence. From the nation which allowed
itself to be deprived of one square mile of
territory by its neighbor, unpunished, the
rest also would be taken, until nothing remained to it to call its own, and it had ceased
to exist as a state; and such a nation would
deserve no better fate.

But if a nation should have recourse to

arms, for the sake of a square mile of territory, without inquiring what its value, why
not also the peasant for the sake of his strip
of land? Or must we dismiss him with the
decree: *quod licet Jovi, non licet bovi.* The
nation does not fight for the square mile of
territory, but for itself, for its honor and
independence; and so in those suits at law
in which the disproportion mentioned above
exists between the value of the object in controversy and the prospective cost and other
sacrifices, there is question not of the insignificant object in controversy, but of an ideal
end: the person's assertion of himself and of
his feeling of right. In respect to this end,
the person whose rights have been invaded
no longer weighs all the sacrifices and incon-
veniences which the suit at law draws after
it — the end in his eyes is compensation for
the means. It is not a mere money-interest
which urges the person whose rights have been
infringed to institute legal proceedings, but
moral pain at the wrong which has been
endured. He is not concerned simply with

28

recovering the object — he may, perhaps, as frequently happens, to prove the real motive in suing, have devoted it from the first to a charitable institution — but with forcing a recognition of his rights. An inner voice tells him that he should not retreat, that it is not the worthless object that is at stake but his own personality, his feeling of legal right, his self-respect — in short, the suit at law ceases to appear to him in the guise of a mere question of interest and becomes a question of character.

But experience teaches us none the less that many others in the same situation come to the very opposite decision — they like peace better than a legal right asserted at the cost of trouble and anxiety. What kind of a judgment must we pass on this? Shall we say simply: That is a matter of individual taste and temperament; one loves contention more, and the other peace; from the standpoint of law both conclusions are to be equally respected; for the law leaves to every one who has a legal right, the choice of asserting his right or of surrendering it. I hold this view, which is to be met with not unfrequently in life, to be reprehensible in the highest degree, and in conflict with the very essence of law. If it were possible that this view should become general, all would be over with the law itself; since whereas the law, to exist, demands that there should be always a manly resistance made to wrong, those who advocate this view preach that the law should flee like a coward before wrong. To this view I oppose the principle: Resistance to injustice, the resistance to wrong in the domain of law, is a duty of all who have legal rights, to themselves—for it is a commandment of moral self-preservation — a duty to the commonwealth;—for this resistance must, in order that the law may assert itself, be universal. I have thus laid down the principle which it is the purpose of the sequel to elaborate.

CHAPTER III

THE STRUGGLE FOR HIS RIGHTS A DUTY OF THE PERSON WHOSE RIGHTS HAVE BEEN VIOLATED, TO HIMSELF

THE struggle for his right is a duty of the person whose rights have been violated, to himself.

The preservation of existence is the highest law of the whole living creation. It manifests itself in every creature in the instinct of self-preservation. Now man is not concerned only with his physical life but with his moral existence. But the condition of this moral existence is right, in the law. In the law, man possesses and defends the moral condition of his existence — without law he sinks to the level of the beast,[1] just as the Romans very logically, from the stand-

[1] In the novel, Michel Kohlhaas, by Heinrich von Kleist, to which I shall return again, the writer makes his hero say: "Better be a dog, if I am to be trodden under foot, than a man."

31

point of abstract law, placed slaves on a level
with beasts. The assertion of one's legal
rights is, therefore, a duty of moral self-
preservation — the total surrender of those
rights, now impossible, but once possible, is
moral suicide. But the law is only the aggregate of its separate parts, each of which
embodies a peculiar moral condition of existence: property as well as marriage, contracts
as well as reputation. A renunciation of
one of them is, therefore, legally just as impossible as the renunciation of the entire law.
But it certainly is possible that a person
should attack one of these conditions; and it
is the duty of the person attacked to repel
the attack: for it is not sufficient to place these
conditions of existence under the protection
of law, represented by mere abstract principles; they must be asserted in the concrete
by the individual; and the incentive to this
assertion of them is furnished when one
arbitrarily dares to attack them.

But not all legal wrong is arbitrariness,
that is a revolt against the idea of law. The

possessor of my chattel who thinks he owns it does not assail my person in denying the idea of property; rather does he appeal to it in his own interest. The question between us turns on this — which of us is the owner? But the thief and the robber place themselves outside the legal domain of property. In my property they deny both the idea of property, and, at the same time, an essential condition of the existence, of my person. If we suppose their mode of action to become general, to become a maxim of the law, property is denied both in theory and in practice. Hence their act embodies an attack, not only on my chattel, but at the same time on my person; and if it be my duty to defend my person, it is my duty here also; and nothing but the conflict of this duty with the higher duty of the preservation of my life, as happens when the robber puts before me the alternative of my money or my life, can justify the abandonment of my property. But leaving this case out of consideration, it is my duty to oppose this disregard of law

33

in my person with all the means at my command. By tolerating that disregard of law, I consent to support injustice for a single moment in my life. But to do this, no one should lend a hand.

Towards the *bonâ fide* possessor of my chattel, I stand in a very different situation. Here the question is what I have to do. It is not a question of my feeling of legal right, of my character, of my personality, but a pure question of interest; for I have nothing here at stake but the value of my chattel, and here, therefore, I am entirely warranted in weighing the gain and stake, and the possibility of a doubtful issue, one against the other, and to come to a decision accordingly: to sue, abstain from suing, or arbitrate.[1] Arbitration or settlement is the point of meeting of such a calculation of probabilities, made

---

1 The above passage should have guarded me from the supposition that I preached the battle for one's legal rights without inquiring further concerning motives and circumstances, and that I considered the surrender of a questionable right as entirely unjustifiable. Only where the person is trampled under foot in his rights have I declared the vindication of one's rights to be a vindication of one's self, and thus a matter of honor and a social duty. When this differ-

by each side, and, with the premises which
I here suppose, it is the best means of closing
the controversy. But if a settlement is often
so difficult to effect; if, as not infrequently
happens, both parties from the first decline
all negotiations tending to a settlement, the
reason is not simply that the calculations of
probabilities by the two parties diverge too
much from each other to be able to meet, but
because each of the parties to the controversy
supposes the other to be consciously wrong,
moved by an evil intent. Thus the question
assumes, even when agitated from the standpoint of a suit at law, under the form of an
objective injustice (*reivindicatio*), psychologi-
cally, for the party, the very same shape as
in the case above — the shape of a conscious
violation of one's right or of law; and the
stubbornness with which the individual here

ence, on which I have laid so much stress, is overlooked, and the
absurd view attributed to me, that wrangling and contention have
something of the beautiful in them, and that litigiousness is a virtue,
I can find no explanation of the fact, except by assuming an evil
intention to set up a view which is not liked in order to refute it, or
a negligence in reading which forgets at the end of the book what
was read in the beginning.

35

defends his rights is based precisely on the same reasons, and is as morally justifiable, as when he defends them against the robber. To wish, in such a case, to deter the party from defending his right, in a suit at law, by pointing out to him the expense and other consequences of the same nature attending it — the uncertainty of the issue, for instance — is a psychological blunder; for the question is, to such a party, not a question of interest, but of his sentiment of justice or of right. The only hope we can cherish here is to cause the supposition of an evil intention to disappear, which caused the party to act; and this done, resistance is overcome; the party may be induced to look at the question in the light of interest, and a settlement or compromise become possible. What stubborn resistance the prepossession and prejudice of the party frequently oppose to all such attempts is only too well known to every practical jurist; and I believe that I shall meet with no contradiction from that quarter when I assert that this inaccessibleness to minds, this tenacious distrust, is a thing not purely individual, determined by the accidental character of the person, but that it is decided by the general differences of education and calling. This distrust is most insurmountable in the case of the peasant. The litigiousness of which he is accused is nothing but the product of two factors especially peculiar to him — a strong sense of property, not to say avarice, and mistrust. No one so well understands his interests, and holds as firmly to what he has, as the peasant; and yet no one so readily sacrifices his fortune to a suit at law. This is apparently a contradiction; but, in reality, it is entirely explainable. Precisely his largely developed sense of property makes an injury to his property all the more sensitively felt, and the reaction, therefore, all the more violent. The litigiousness of the peasant is nothing but the aberration of the sense of property, produced by mistrust, an aberration which, like the analogous phenomenon in love, jealousy, aims its dart at itself, inasmuch as it destroys what it seeks to save.

37

The old Roman law affords an interesting confirmation of what I have just now said. This mistrust of the peasant, which, in every conflict of law, supposes an evil intention in one's opponent, finds expression in that law in the form of legal principles. Everywhere, even where there is question of a conflict of law in which each of the contending parties may be in good faith, the defeated party has to pay a penalty for his resistance. The simple restoration to a person of his rights is no satisfaction to the outraged feeling of right. The defeated party, whether innocent or guilty, had to make satisfaction for having opposed the law.[1] If our peasants to-day had the making of the law, it would, we may conjecture, be very like that of their old Roman predecessors. But even in Rome, this mistrust in law was in principle overcome by civilization, inasmuch as two sorts of injustice were distinguished, the guilty and the innocent, or the subjective and objective (in the language of Hegel, the ingenuous wrong).

[1] I shall return to this later.

38

This distinction between objective and subjective injustice is, from a legislative and
scientific point of view, a very important one.
It expresses the manner in which the law looks
upon the matter, and it justifies the consequences which the violation of law draws after
it. But it does not at all decide how the
individual shall look upon it; how his feeling
of legal right will be excited by an injustice
done him, a feeling which does not pulsate
in accordance with the abstract notions of
the system. The circumstances of the case
may be such that the person whose rights
have been violated may have every reason,
in a conflict about rights, which, according
to the law, falls under the head of an objective
violation of law, to proceed on the assumption
of an evil intent, of conscious injustice on the
part of his opponent; and this judgment of
his, will rightly decide what his course towards
his opponent should be. The fact that the
law gives me the very same *condictio ex mutuo*
against the heir of my debtor who knows
nothing of the debt, and makes the payment

39

of it dependent on the proof, as against the debtor himself, who shamelessly denies the loan made him, or refuses to pay it without reason, cannot keep me from looking at the mode of action of the two in an entirely different light, and to frame my own action accordingly. The debtor himself is to me on the same footing as the thief. He knowingly tries to deprive me of what is mine. It is the rising up of caprice against law, only it is in a situation to clothe itself in a legal garb. The heir of the debtor, on the other hand, is like the *bonâ fide* possessor of what belongs to me. He does not deny the principle that the debtor must pay, but only the assertion that he is a debtor himself, and all that I have said above of the *bonâ fide* possessor applies to him. With him I may settle or compromise. I may, in his case, desist entirely from the institution of a suit; but, as against the debtor, I should and I must follow up my right, cost what it may. Not to do this would be to admit the debtor to be right, —nay, more, to abandon the right.

I suppose that it will be objected to what I have thus far said: what do the people know of the right of property, of contract as a moral condition of the existence of the person? *Know?* They may know nothing about it, but whether they do not feel it is another question; and I hope that I shall be able to show that such is the case. What do the people know of the kidneys, lungs, liver, as conditions of their physical life? But every one feels the stitch in the lungs, or a pain in the kidneys or liver, and understands the warning which it conveys to him. Physical pain is the signal of a disturbance in the organism, of the presence of an influence inimical to it. It opens our eyes to an impending danger, and compels us, by the pain which it causes, to oppose it in time. The very same is true of the moral pain caused us by intentional injustice, by arbitrariness. Varying in intensity, just like the physical, according to the difference of subjective sensitiveness, of the form and object of the injustice (on which more anon), it manifests

itself also in every individual not entirely
blunted to it, *i.e.*, in every individual who
has not grown accustomed to positive lawlessness, as moral pain, and thus summons
him to fight against the cause which produces
it — not so much to put an end to the feeling
of pain as to preserve the health, which is
threatened by the inactive bearing of it. It
is a reminder of the duty of moral self-preservation, such as physical pain is in respect to
physical self-preservation.

Let us take the most undoubted case, an
attack on one's honor, and the profession in
which it is most sensitively developed — the
military profession. An officer who has patiently borne an insult which involves his
honor is no longer an officer. Why? The
vindication of his honor is every man's duty.
Why then does the military gentleman attach
more importance than any other to the ful-
fillment of this duty? Because he has the
right feeling, that the courageous vindication
of one's personality is, for him, more, perhaps,
than for a person of any other class, an indis-

pensable condition of his order, which, in its very nature, should be the incorporation of personal courage, and which cannot endure the cowardice of its members without sacrificing itself. With the officer, let us now compare the peasant, who defends his property with the greatest stubbornness, but evinces a surprising indifference as to his honor. Why? Because he, too, has a correct feeling of the peculiar conditions of his existence. He is not called upon to give proof of his courage, but to work. His property is only the visible form which his labor in the past has taken. The lazy peasant, who takes no care of his land or who dissipates his little fortune, is as much despised by other peasants as is the officer who lightly values his honor, by his colleagues. But one peasant will never reproach another because he has not fought a duel, or instituted a suit to avenge an insult; nor one officer another, because he has mismanaged his property. The piece of land which he tills, the cattle which he raises, are to the peasant the basis of his entire existence; and the angry lawsuit which he institutes against the neighbor who has deprived him of a few feet of land, or against the trader who refuses to pay him for the oxen which he has sold him, is only his way of doing what the officer does with his sword—of battling for his rights. Both sacrifice themselves without reserve. They leave the consequences of their action entirely out of consideration. And this they must do, for, in doing it, they are only obeying the peculiar law of their moral self-preservation. Put them in the jury-box—submit to a jury of officers the case of an injury to property, and to a jury of peasants a question of honor —and see how different their verdicts! It is well known that there are no severer judges, in the matter of injuries to property, than the peasantry. And although I cannot here speak from experience, I have no manner of doubt that if a peasant were to bring an action for damages for assault and battery, for instance, it would be found much easier to induce him to arbitrate than if his action

44

were for an injury to property. The old Roman peasant was satisfied with twenty-five *as* for a slap on the face; and when a person put out one of his eyes, he was willing to talk the matter over and to arbitrate, instead of putting out one of his opponent's eyes, as he was authorized to do. But he demanded that the law should empower him to hold the thief caught in the act, as a slave, and, in case of resistance, to slay him; and the law permitted him to do so. In the former case, only his honor, his body, was at stake; in the latter, his property.

As a third illustration, let us take the case of the merchant. His credit is to him what honor is to the officer, and property to the peasant. The maintenance of his credit is, for him, a vital question; and the man who charges him with negligence in meeting his obligations deals him a heavier blow than the one who attacks his person or robs him. It is in keeping with this peculiar position of the merchant that recent laws tend more and more to restrict the crime of negligent and fraudulent bankruptcy, to him and others like him.

By what I have just said I have not intended simply to show that the irritability of the feeling of legal right varies according to class and calling, inasmuch as that feeling measures the wounding character of the injury in accordance with the interest which the class, as a class, has not to endure it. The proof of this fact serves only to place in its true light the truth of a much higher order, that every man possessed of a legal right defends the moral conditions of his existence when he defends his legal right. For the fact that the feeling of legal right shows itself most irritable, in the case of the three classes named, in the points in which we have recognized the conditions of existence of these classes peculiarly to reside, proves that the reaction of the feeling of legal right is not like that of feelings generally, determined only by the temperament and character of the individual, but that it is determined likewise by a social cause; viz., the feeling of the indispensableness of this very branch of the law to the vital end of the particular class. The degree of energy with which the feeling of legal right reacts against an infringement of legal right is, in my eyes, a sure measure of the importance which individuals, a class or people, really attach, both to the law in general and to a special branch of it, for themselves and their special aim in life. This principle I hold to be universally true, true in the case of public as well as of private law. The same irritability which the different classes manifest in respect to a violation of all those legal provisions which, in a special manner, constitute the basis of their existence, we find also in the case of states, in respect to those institutions in which the peculiar principle of their life seems realized. The measure of their irritability, and of the value which they attach to these heads of the law, is found in the criminal law. The surprising difference which prevails in criminal law (*Strafrecht*—penal justice), in respect to severity and mildness, is accounted

47

for, in great part, by the principle mentioned above, of the conditions of existence. Every state punishes those crimes most severely which threaten its own peculiar condition of existence, while it allows a moderation to prevail in regard to other crimes which, not infrequently, presents a very striking contrast to its severity as against the former. A theocracy brands blasphemy and idolatry as crimes deserving of death, while it looks upon a boundary violation as a simple misdemeanor. (Mosaic law.) The agricultural state, on the other hand, visits the latter with the severest punishment, while it lets the blasphemer go with the lightest punishment. (Old Roman law.) The commercial state punishes most severely the uttering of false coin, the military state insubordination and breach of official duty, the absolute state high treason, the republic the striving after regal power; and they all manifest a severity in these points which contrasts greatly with the manner in which they punish other crimes. In short, the reaction of the feeling of legal

48

right, both of states and individuals, is most violent when they feel themselves threatened in the conditions of existence peculiar to them.[1]

Just as the peculiar conditions of a class or calling invest certain heads of the law with an enhanced importance, and thus enhance the sensitiveness of the feelings of legal right in respect to a violation of them, these same conditions may also produce a weakening of that sentiment. The servant-class cannot maintain and develop the feeling of honor among themselves as do the other strata of society. Their position brings with it certain humiliations, against which a single servant revolts in vain, so long as the class itself endures them. An individual with a sensitive feeling of honor, in such a situation, has no alternative but to lower his claims to the level of those of his like or to give up the calling. Only when such a way of feeling becomes general is there any prospect for the individual, instead of wasting his strength in a useless

[1] The learned know that I have here only turned to account ideas, the merit of having recognized and formulated which belongs to the great *Montesquieu*, "Esprit des Lois".

struggle, to turn it to account, in union with
those who think as he does, to raise the level
of the honor of his class; and I mean here,
not simply the subjective feeling of honor, but
its objective recognition by the other classes
of society and by legislation. The history
of the social development of the last fifty
years shows immense progress in this direction. What I have just said might have been
applied half a century ago to most classes.
The enhanced feeling of honor to be found in
them is only the result and the expression of
the legal position which they have secured.

What I have said above of honor is true
also of property. The sensitiveness of the
feeling of legal right in relation to property,
the real sense of property — I mean here not
the instinct of acquisition, the hunting after
money and wealth, but the manly feeling of
the owner, as the model representative of
whom I have chosen the peasant, of the
owner who defends what belongs to him, not
because it is an object of value, but because
it belongs to him — this feeling, this sense of

property, also may become enfeebled under
the unhealthy influence of causes and circumstances. What, we hear a great many
ask, has the thing which belongs to me, to
do with my person, with me? It serves me
as a means of subsistence, of acquisition, of
enjoyment; but as there is no moral duty incumbent on me to amass a great deal of money,
there can be no duty incumbent on me to go
to law for a mere trifle, at a great expenditure
of time and money, and at the sacrifice of my
rest. The only motive which urges me to
go to law to assert my right to my property is
the motive which determines me to acquire
it, and which determines the disposition I shall
make of it — my interest. Whether I shall
go to law to assert my right to my property,
or not, is simply a question of interest.

For my part, in such a view, I can see only
a degeneration of the true sense of property,
the reason of which seems to me to be a dis-
placement, an ignoring, of its natural basis.
I do not hold wealth and luxury responsible
for this degeneration — in neither of them do

I discover any danger to the feeling of legal
right of the people — but the love of gain
grown immoral. The historical source and
ethical justification of property is labor —
the labor not of the hand or arm alone, but
of the mind and of talent; and I acknowledge
the right, not only of the workman himself
to the product of his labor, but of his heir
also; that is, I discover in the right of inheritance a necessary consequence of the principle
of labor; for I maintain that the laborer
should not be prevented denying himself the
enjoyment of his property and leaving it to
another, whether during his lifetime or after
his death. Only through a lasting connection with labor can property maintain itself
fresh and healthy. Only at this source is it
seen, clearly and transparently, to the very
bottom, to be what it is to man. The further
the stream is removed from this, its source,
and winds into the devious direction of easy
and toilless gain, the more turbid do its waters
become, until, in the slime of speculation on
'Change and of fraudulent stock-jobbing, it

loses every trace of what it was in its origin. At that point every vestige of the moral idea of property has departed, and there can be no longer question of the moral duty of de-fending it. Here there can no longer be any understanding of the meaning of property as it exists in the breast of the man who has to earn his bread in the sweat of his brow. The worst of all is, that the opinions and habits generated by such causes unfortunately gradually extend to circles in which they would not have appeared spontaneously without contagious contact.[1] The influence of the millions won by stock-jobbing extends even to the poor man's hut; and the same person who, in another environment, would have tasted, in his own experience, the bless-ings of labor, feels that same labor, under the enervating pressure of such an atmosphere, a curse, and only a curse. Communism thrives only in those quagmires in which the

[1] An interesting proof of this is furnished by the small German university cities, supported mainly by students. The manner in which these think and act in the matter of spending money is invol-untarily communicated to the population.

true idea of property is lost. At the source of the stream it is not to be found. We may verify in the country, in a directly opposite sense, this fact of experience: that the manner in which the ruling classes look at property is not confined to the latter, but that it is communicated to the other classes of society. The person permanently living in the country, who does not keep entirely aloof from the peasantry, will involuntarily, and even when not urged thereto by his circumstances or his own peculiar character, take up something of the peasant's frugality and sense of property. The same average man, under otherwise entirely similar circumstances, will be economical with the peasant in the country, and a spendthrift with the millionaire in a city like Vienna.

But whatever may be the cause of that weakness of character which the love of ease induces to evade the struggle for legal right, all we have to do here is to recognize it and to describe it as it is. What is the practical philosophy of life which it preaches but the

policy of the coward? The coward who
flees the battle saves what others sacrifice—
his life; but he saves it at the cost of his honor.
Only the fact that others make a stand
protects him and the community from the
consequences which his mode of action would
otherwise inevitably draw after it. If all
thought as he, they would all be lost. And
precisely the same is true of the cowardly
abandonment of one's legal rights. Innocent
as the act of an individual, it would, if raised
to the dignity of a general principle of action,
be the destruction of the entire law. And
even under these circumstances, the apparent absence of danger in such a mode of action
is possible only because the struggle of law
against wrong is, on the whole, not affected
by it any further. For, indeed, it is not
individuals alone who are called upon to take
part in this struggle, but, in organized states,
the state-power also takes a very large part
in it, inasmuch as it prosecutes and punishes
all serious attacks on the life, liberty or
property of the individual, of its own motion,

thus relieving him of the hardest part of the work. But even in respect to those violations of law, the prosecution of which is left entirely to the individual, care is taken that the struggle may not be interrupted; for every one does not follow the policy of the coward, and even the latter takes his place in the line of combatants, at least when the value of the object in controversy outweighs his ease. But let us suppose a state of things in which the protection afforded by the police power and by the criminal law is wanting; let us transfer ourselves to a time when, as in ancient Rome, the pursuit of the thief and the robber was the affair only of the person injured, and who does not see to what such an abandonment of one's legal rights would have led? To what would it have conduced but to the encouragement of thieves and robbers? The very same thing is true of the life of nations. Here each nation is thrown entirely on its own resources. No higher power relieves it of the necessity of asserting its rights, and I need only recall the example given above of the square mile, to show what that view of life which would measure the resistance to wrong according to the material value of the object in controversy, means to the life of nations. But a principle which, wherever tested, proves itself completely unthinkable, the dissolution and destruction of the law, cannot, even where, by way of exception, its fatal consequences are paralyzed by other circumstances, be called correct. I shall have occasion to show later what a disastrous influence such a principle exerts, even under such relatively favorable circumstances.

Let us, therefore, reject this morality of convenience and ease, which no nation and no individual, with a healthy feeling of legal right, has ever adopted. It is the sign and the product of a diseased feeling of legal right; it is coarse and naked materialism, in the domain of law. Even materialism has, within certain limits, its *raison d'être* in this domain. To profit by one's legal rights, to make use of them and to assert them when there is question of a purely objective wrong, is only a question of interest; and a legal right according to the definition which I have given of it myself,[1] is nothing but an interest protected by the law. But in the presence of arbitrariness which lifts its hand against the law, this material consideration loses all value, for the blow which it aims at my legal right, strikes my person also when it strikes the law.

It is a matter of indifference what the object of the right is. If mere chance were to put me in possession of an object, I might be deprived of it without any injury to my person, but it is not chance, but my will, which establishes a bond between myself and it, and even my will only at the price of the past labor of myself or of another;— it is a part of my own strength and of my own past, or of the strength and past of another, which I possess and assert in it. In making it my own, I stamped it with the mark of my own person; whoever attacks it, attacks me; the

[1] "Geist des röm. R." iii, p. 60.

blow dealt it strikes me, for I am present in it. Property is but the periphery of my person extended to things.

This connection of the law with the person invests all rights, no matter what their nature, with that incommensurable value which, in opposition to their purely material value, I call *ideal value*. From it springs that devotedness and energy in the assertion of legal right which I have described above. This ideal conception of the law is not a privilege of characters highly endowed by nature; but it is as accessible to the coarsest as to the most cultured, to the richest as to the poorest, to savage and to civilized nations; and, just here, we discover so clearly how firmly rooted in the innermost nature of the law this idealism is — it is nothing but the healthfulness of the feeling of legal right. The law which, on the one hand, seems to relegate man exclusively to the low region of egotism and interest, lifts him, on the other hand, to an ideal height, in which he forgets all policy, all calculation, that measure of

interest which he had learned to apply everywhere, in order to sacrifice himself purely
and simply in the defense of an idea. Law
which, in the former region, is prose, becomes,
in the struggle for law, poetry in the latter;
for the struggle for law, the battle for one's
legal rights, is the poetry of character.

What is it, then, that works this wonder?
Not knowledge, not education, but simply
the feeling of pain. Pain is the cry of dis-
tress, the call for help of imperiled nature.
This is true, as I have already remarked,
both of the moral and the physical organism;
and what the pathology of the human organism is to the physician, the pathology of the
feeling of legal right is to the jurist and the
philosopher in the sphere of law; or, rather,
it is what it should be to them, for it would
be wrong to say that it is such to them
already. In it, in truth, lies the whole secret
of the law. The pain which a person experiences when his legal rights are violated is
the spontaneous, instinctive admission, wrung
from him by force, of what the law is to him

as an individual, in the first place, and then of what it is to human society. In this one moment, and in the form of an emotion, of direct feeling, we see more of the real meaning and nature of the law than during long years of undisturbed enjoyment. The man who has not experienced this pain himself, or observed it in others, knows nothing of what law is, even if he had committed the whole *corpus juris* to memory. Not the intellect, but the feeling, is able to answer this question; and hence language has rightly designated the psychological source of all law as the *feeling of legal right* (*Rechtsgefühl*). The consciousness of legal right (*Rechtsbewusstsein*), legal conviction, are scientific abstractions with which the people are not acquainted. The power of the law lies in feeling, just as does the power of love; and the intellect cannot supply that feeling when it is wanting. But as love frequently does not know itself, and as a single instant suffices to bring it to a full consciousness of itself, so the feeling of legal right uniformly knows not what it is,

61

and what it can do, so long as it is not wounded; but the violation of legal right compels it to speak, unveils the truth, and manifests its force. I have already said in what this truth consists. His legal right, the law, is the moral condition of existence of the person; the assertion of that right is his moral self-preservation.

The force with which the feeling of legal right reacts, when wounded, is the test of its health. The degree of pain which it experiences tells it what value it attaches to the imperiled goods. But to experience the pain without taking to heart its warning to ward off the impending danger, to bear it patiently and take no measure of defense, is a denial of the feeling of legal right, excusable, perhaps, under certain circumstances, in a particular case, but impossible in the long run without the most disastrous consequences to the feeling of legal right itself. For the essence of that feeling is action. Where it does not act, it languishes and becomes blunted, until finally it grows almost insensible to pain.

Irritability, that is the capacity to feel pain at the violation of one's legal rights, and action, that is the courage and the determination to repel the attack, are, in my eyes, the two criteria of a healthy feeling of legal right.

I must refrain from elaborating any further this interesting and instructive subject of the pathology of the feeling of legal right; but I would, however, ask permission to make a few remarks just here.

The sensitiveness of the feeling of legal right, otherwise the sentiment of law, is not the same in all individuals, but it increases and decreases according as, and to the extent that, each individual class or people experiences the law as a moral condition of existence; and not the law in general only, but its several parts. This I have shown above, in reference to property and reputation. As a third example, I may here add, marriage. What reflections does not the manner in which different individuals, nations, codes of law, look at adultery, suggest!

The second element in the feeling of legal

63

right, action, is a mere matter of character:
the attitude which an individual or a nation
assumes towards an attempt on its rights
is the surest test of its character. If by
character we understand personality, full,
self-reliant and self-asserting, there can be
no better opportunity to test this quality
than when arbitrariness attacks one's rights,
and, with his rights, his person. The manner
in which the wounded feeling of law or of
personality reacts, whether under the influence of passion in wild and violent action, or
with subdued, persistent resistance, is no
measure of the intensity of the strength of
the sentiment of legal right; and there can
be no greater error than to ascribe to the
savage or the uncultured man, with whom
the former manner is the normal one, a strong-
er feeling of legal right, than to the educated
man who takes the second course. This
manner is more or less a matter of education
and temperament; but a firm, tenacious and
resolute resistance is in no way inferior to
violent and passionate reaction. It would

be deplorable if it were otherwise. Were it otherwise, individuals and nations would lose the feeling of legal right in proportion as they advanced in culture. A glance at history and at everyday life is sufficient to show that this is not the case. Nor is the answer to be found in the contrast of rich and poor. Different as is the measure with which the rich man and the poor man measure the value of things, it is not at all applied in the case of a violation of legal right; for here the question is not the material value of a thing, but the ideal value of a legal right, the energy of the feeling of legal right in relation to property; and hence it is not the amount of property, but the strength of the feeling of legal right, which here decides the issue. The best proof of this is afforded by the English people. Their wealth has caused no detriment to their feeling of legal right; and what energy it still possesses, even in pure questions of property, we, on the Continent, have frequently proof enough of, in the typical figure of the traveling Englishman who resists being duped by inn-keepers and hackmen with a manfulness which would induce one to think he was defending the law of Old England — who, in case of need, postpones his departure, remains days in the place and spends ten times the amount he refuses to pay. The people laugh at him, and do not understand him. It were better if they did understand him. For, in the few shillings which the man here defends, Old England lives. At home, in his own country, every one understands him, and no one lightly ventures to overreach him. Place an Austrian of the same social position and the same means in the place of the Englishman — how would he act? If I can trust my own experience in this matter, not one in ten would follow the example of the Englishman. Others shun the disagreeableness of the controversy, the making of a sensation, the possibility of a misunderstanding to which they might expose themselves, a misunderstanding which the Englishman in England need not at all fear, and which he quietly takes into the

66

bargain: that is, they pay. But in the few pieces of silver which the Englishman refuses and which the Austrian pays there lies concealed more than one would think, of England and Austria; there lie concealed centuries of their political development and of their social life.

CHAPTER IV

THE ASSERTION OF ONE'S RIGHTS A DUTY TO SOCIETY

THUS far I have endeavored to establish the first of the principles laid down above, that the struggle for law is a duty of the person having rights, to himself. I now turn to the second; viz., that the assertion of one's legal rights is a duty which he owes to society.

To establish this principle, it is necessary that I should examine somewhat more closely the relation of law in the objective sense to law in the subjective sense of the term. In what does the relation consist? I state, I believe, the theory admitted in our days, accurately, when I say that it consists in this: that the former is the condition precedent of the latter. A concrete legal right exists only where the conditions are to be found which the abstract principle of law has attached to its being. When we have said this, we have, according to the prevailing theory, completely exhausted their relation to one another. But this view is altogether one-sided. It lays stress exclusively on the dependence of the concrete law on the abstract, but overlooks the fact that there is, just as much, a similar relation of dependence in the opposite direction. Concrete law not only receives life and strength from abstract law, but gives it back, in turn, the life it has received. It is of the nature of the law to be realized in practice. A principle of law never applied in practice, or which has lost its force, no longer deserves the name; it is a worn-out spring in the machinery of the law, which performs no service and which may be removed without changing its action in the least. This applies without limitation to all parts of the law — to the law of nations as well as to private and criminal law; and the Roman law has given it its express sanction, inasmuch as it considers *desuetudo* as an abrogation of a law. This *desuetudo* corresponds to loss of concrete legal rights by non-user (*non-usus*). But while the realization in practice of public law and of criminal law is assured, because it is imposed as a duty on public officials, the realization in practice of private law is presented to individuals under the form of their legal rights; that is, it is left exclusively to them to take the initiative in its realization, left exclusively to their action. In the former case, its practical realization depends on the performance of their duty by the authorities and public officials, and, in this latter case, on the assertion by individuals of their legal rights. If the latter, for any reason, neglect to assert their rights, permanently and generally, be it from ignorance, love of ease, or fear, the consequence is that the principles of right lose their vigor. And so we may say: The reality, the practical force of the principles of private law, is proved by the assertion of concrete legal right; and as, on the one hand, the latter receives its life from the laws, it, on the other, gives back life to the laws; the relation of objective or abstract legal right and subjective or concrete legal right is the circulation of the blood, which flows from the heart and returns to the heart.

The existence of all the principles of public law depends on the fidelity of public officials in the performance of their duties; that of the principles of private law, on the power of the motives which induce the person whose rights have been violated to defend them: his interest and his sentiment of legal right. If these motives do not come into play, if the feeling of legal right is blunted and weak, and interest not powerful enough to overcome the disinclination to entering into a controversy and the indisposition to go to law, the consequence is that the principle of law involved finds no application.

But, we shall be asked, what matters it? No one suffers from this but the person whose rights have been invaded. I must again have recourse to the illustration already used, of the individual who flees the battle. If there

are a thousand men in the fight, the defection
of one may make no difference; but if a hundred of them desert their colors, the position
of those who remain faithful becomes more
and more perilous; the whole weight of the
battle falls on them alone. This, it seems to
me, is a correct representation of the state
of the question. In the domain of private
law also, there is a question of a struggle of
legal right against injustice, of a common
struggle of the whole nation, in which all
should cling together. Desertion, in such a
case, is treason to the common cause, for it
strengthens the common enemy by increasing
his boldness and audacity. When arbitrariness and audacity boldly dare to lift their
head, it is always a sure sign that those who
are called to defend the law have not done
their duty. But each of us, in his own place,
is called upon to defend the law, to guard and
enforce it in his own sphere. The concrete
legal right which belongs to him is only his
authorization by the state to enter the lists
when his interests require it, for the law, and

to ward off injustice — a call made upon
him which is partial and limited, in contra-
distinction to that made upon the public
official, which is absolute and unlimited. In
defending his legal rights he asserts and
defends the whole body of law, within the
narrow space which his own legal rights occupy.
Hence his interest, and this, his mode of
action, extend far beyond his own person.
The general good which results therefrom is
not only the ideal interest, that the authority
and majesty of the law are protected, but this
other very real and eminently practical good
which every one feels and understands, even
the person who has no conception whatever
of the former — that the established order
of social relations is defended and assured.
When the master can no longer insist that
the servant shall do his duty, when the creditor cannot enforce payment by his debtor,
when the public attach no great importance
to the correctness of weights and measures,
can it be said that nothing is imperiled but
the authority of the law? When these things

74

come to pass, the order of civil life is sacrificed in one direction, and it is not easy to say how far the disastrous consequences produced may reach; whether, for instance, the whole system of credit may not be seriously affected thereby. For every man will do all in his power to have nothing to do with people who force him to wrangle and struggle where his legal right is clear; and he will transfer his capital to other places and order his goods elsewhere.

Under such circumstances, the lot of the few who have the courage to enforce the law becomes a real martyrdom. Their strong feeling of legal right, which will not permit them to quit the field, becomes a curse to them. Forsaken by all who should have been their natural allies, they stand alone against the lawlessness which has grown up in consequence of universal indolence and cowardice; and if, after all their sacrifices, they earn the satisfaction of having remained true to themselves, they reap, instead of gratitude, ridicule and scorn. The responsibility for this state of things falls not upon those who transgress the law, but on those who have not the courage to assert it. Do not accuse injustice of usurping the place of the law, but the law of permitting that usurpation. If I were called upon to pass judgment on the practical importance of the two principles: "Do no injustice," and: "Suffer no injustice," I would say that the first rule was: Suffer no injustice, and the second: Do none! If we take man as he actually is, there is no doubt that the certainty of meeting a firm and resolute resistance is far more powerful to prevent the commission of an injustice, than a simple prohibition which has, in fact, no greater practical force than a moral precept.

After all this, can I be charged with claiming too much when I say: The defense of one's concrete legal rights, when these rights are attacked, is a duty of the individual whose rights have been invaded, not only to himself, but also to society? If what I have said be true, that in defending his legal right he, at the same time, defends the law, and in the

law that public order which is indispensable,
who can deny that, in defending them, he
fulfills a duty to the commonwealth? If
the latter may summon him to fight a foreign
enemy and to risk his life in battle with him;
if it be every one's duty to defend the common
interests of the country, when attacked from
without, why should not all courageous and
well-minded men unite to resist the enemy
at home? And if, in the former case, cowardly
flight is considered treason to the common
cause, why is it not treason in the latter also?
Law and justice cannot thrive in a country
simply because the judge sits always ready
on the bench, and the agents of the police
power are ever at its command. That they
may thrive, every member of society must
co-operate with these. Every one is called
upon, and it is every one's duty, to crush the
hydra-head of arbitrariness and lawlessness,
whenever they show it. Every man who
enjoys the blessings of the law should also
contribute his share to maintain the power
of the law and respect for the law. Every

man is a born battler for the law in the interest of society.

I do not need to call attention to the extent to which the vocation of the individual to assert his legal right is ennobled when it is viewed in this way. Our actual theory tells us only of a purely passive attitude towards the law; the doctrine here advocated puts in its place one of reciprocity, in which the person with legal rights returns to the law the service which he receives from it. Our doctrine thus looks upon him as a collaborator in a great national work. Whether the person himself looks upon it in this way is a matter of no moment. For the grand and the sublime in the moral order of the world is that it can count on the services not only of those who comprehend it, but that it possesses efficacious means enough to make those who do not understand its commands labor for it without their knowledge or their will. To force men to engage in the matrimonial relation, it brings into play, in the case of some men, the noblest of all human

78

instincts, in the case of others sensual pleasure, in a third case convenience, in a fourth covetousness — but all these motives lead to marriage. And so, in the struggle for law, interest calls one to the scene of strife, pain at the spectacle of violated legal right another, the idea of law a third — they all lend each other a hand in the common work, opposition to arbitrariness.

We have now reached the ideal height of the struggle for law. Rising from the lower motive of interest we have lifted ourselves to the point of view of the moral self-preservation of the person and finally come to co-operation in the realization of the idea of law.

In my rights the law was violated and denied. In my rights it is defended, asserted and restored. What an immense importance does the struggle of the individual for his rights thus obtain! How far below the height of this ideal, universal interest in the law, lies the sphere of that which is purely individual, the region of personal interests,

79

aims, and passions which the uncultured man looks upon as the real domain of the law!

But that height, many may say, is so great that it is visible only to the eyes of the philosophy of law; it is never thought of in practical life; no one institutes an action for the sake of the idea of law. To refute this statement, I might refer to the Roman law, in which the actuality of this ideal view is attested most clearly by the existence of the popular actions,[1] but we would be doing ourselves a

[1]I would remark, for the benefit of those of my readers who have not studied law, that these suits (*actiones populares*) afforded an opportunity to all who desired it to appear as representatives of the law and to bring those who had violated it to account; and not only where there was question of the public interest, and consequently also of that of the accuser, but wherever an individual whose rights had been violated was not in a way to defend himself fully, as, for instance, when a minor had been wronged in a contract of sale, or where a tutor had been unfaithful to his pupil, etc. See my "Geist des röm. Rechts," *iii*, *p. 107.* These actions, therefore, involved an appeal to the ideal feeling which defends the law because it is the law, and not on account of any personal interest. Others of these actions appealed to the ordinary motive of cupidity, by causing the accuser to hope for the fine imposed on the accused, and hence it is that the same stain attached to them, or rather to their institution for gain, which among us attaches to informers. When I add that the actions of the second class mentioned above disappeared in the later Roman law, and that those of the first have disappeared in our own, every reader will be able to draw the correct conclusion from these premises; viz., that the conditions which they supposed had disappeared.

great injustice, if we were to deny that we also possessed this ideal feeling. Every man who sees the law violated and feels indignation at the sight, possesses it. While, in fact, an egotistical motive is mixed up with the painful feeling caused by a personal wrong, this indignation is produced exclusively by the power of morality over the human heart. It is the energy of our moral nature protesting against the violation of the law; it is the most beautiful and the highest testimony which the feeling of legal right can bear to itself; it is a moral phenomenon which calls for the study of the psychologist and appeals to the imagination of the poet. No other feeling, so far as I know, is able so suddenly, so radically, to make a change in man; for it is a demonstrated fact that it has the power to rouse the gentlest and most conciliating natures to a pitch of passion which is otherwise entirely foreign to them; a fact which proves that they have been wounded in the noblest part of their being and touched in its most sensitive fibres. It is the phenom-

enon of the storm in the moral world: sublime,
majestic in the rapidity, suddenness, and
power with which it breaks forth, in the
strength of that moral force, which like a
tempest or the elements in a fury, sweeps
everything before it, then grows calm and
beneficent, and produces a purification of
the moral atmosphere enjoyed both by the
individual and by all. But if the limited
power of the individual spends itself in vain
against institutions which afford a protection
to lawlessness which they refuse to right, it
is plain that the storm recoils on the head of
its author; and then one of two things: either
his wounded feeling of legal right will make of
him one of those criminals of whom I shall
speak further on, or he will afford us the no
less tragical spectacle of a man who, ever
bearing in his breast the sting which injustice
that he has not been able to resist, has left
there, gradually loses his moral life and all
faith in the law.

I readily grant that this ideal sentiment of
legal right, possessed by the person by whom

the wounding of the feeling of legal right is felt more sensitively than an attack upon him personally, and who disinterestedly sacrifices himself in the interest of oppressed right as if there were question only of his own rights, is the privilege of highly gifted natures. However, even the cold feeling of legal right, destitute of all idealism, which is affected only by the wrong done to itself, fully understands the relation between concrete legal right and the law, which I have demonstrated and summed up thus: My legal right is the law; when my legal right is violated, the law is violated; when it is asserted, the law is asserted. It sounds paradoxical, and yet it is true, that precisely among jurists this view is far from being usual. According to their view, in the struggle for concrete legal rights, the law itself is in no way involved; the struggle does not turn on the abstract law, but on its incorporation in the form of this concrete legal right, a photograph, so to speak, of that law, in which it has become fixed, but in which it is not itself directly affected. I do not intend to question the technical necessity of this view, but it should not keep us from acknowledging the correctness of the opposed view, which places the law on the same level with concrete legal right, and sees in the imperiling of the latter the imperiling of the former also. To the unprejudiced feeling of right, the latter view, it seems to me, must commend itself much more strongly than the former. The best proof of what I here allege is the expression which the Germans employ, and which was used in the Latin. In a case at law, the plaintiff is said in Germany to invoke the law (*das Gesetz anrufen*); the Romans called the complaint *legis actio*. The law itself is called in question; it is the law itself which is under discussion in a particular case — a view of the highest importance for the understanding of the old Roman process, *legis actio*. Hence the struggle for one's legal rights is, at the same time, a struggle for the law. There is question not alone of a personal interest, of a single relation in which the law has been incorporated, of a photographic picture, as I have called it, in which a transient ray of the law has perpetuated itself, and which may be broken up and divided without affecting the law; but there is a question of the law itself which has been despised, trampled under foot, and which must be defended, if the law itself is not to become a mockery and a word without meaning. When the legal right of the individual is sacrificed, the law is sacrificed likewise.

This view, which I may call the solidarity of the law with concrete legal right, is, as I have shown above, the real expression of their relations in their most intimate nature. It is not, however, so very obscure but that the mere egotist, incapable of entertaining an elevated idea, may catch it. On the contrary, it may be the one which he understands the most readily, for his interest is to associate himself with the state in the struggle. And thus even he is, without his knowledge or his will, lifted above himself and his legal right to that ideal social eminence where he becomes the representative of the law. The truth remains truth, even when the individual defends it only from the narrow point of view of his personal interest. It is hatred and revenge that take Shylock before the court to cut his pound of flesh out of Antonio's body; but the words which the poet puts into his mouth are as true in it as in any other. It is the language which the wounded feeling of legal right will speak, at all times and in all places; the power, the firmness of the conviction, that law must remain law, the lofty feeling and pathos of a man who is conscious that, in what he claims, there is question not only of his person but of the law. "The pound of flesh," Shakespeare makes him say:—

> "The pound of flesh, which I demand of him,
> Is dearly bought, is mine, and I will have it;
> If you deny me, fie upon your law;
> There is no force in the decrees of Venice.
> . . . . . I crave the law.
> . . . . . I stay here upon my bond."

"I crave the law." In these four words, the poet has described the relation of law in

86

the subjective, to law in the objective sense
of the term and the meaning of the struggle
for law, in a manner better than any philosopher of the law could have done it. These
four words change Shylock's claim into a
question of the law of Venice. To what
mighty, giant dimensions does not the weak
man grow, when he speaks these words!
It is no longer the Jew demanding his pound
of flesh; it is the law of Venice itself knocking
at the door of Justice; for his rights and the
law of Venice are one and the same; they both
stand or fall together. And when he finally
succumbs under the weight of the judge's
decision, who wipes out his rights by a shocking
piece of pleasantry,[1] when we see him pursued

[1] The eminently tragic interest which we feel in Shylock, I find to
have its basis precisely in the fact that justice is not done him; for
this is the conclusion to which the lawyer must come. The poet is,
of course, free to build up his own system of jurisprudence, and we
have no reason to regret that Shakespeare has done so here; or
rather that he has changed the old fable in nothing. But when the
jurist submits the question to a critical examination, he can only say
that the bond was in itself null and void because its provisions were
contrary to good morals. The judge should, therefore, have refused
to enforce its terms on this ground from the first. But as he did not
do so, as the "wise Daniel" admitted its validity, it was a wretched
subterfuge, a miserable piece of pettifoggery, to deny the man whose

by bitter scorn, bowed, broken, tottering on his way, who can help feeling that in him the law of Venice is humbled; that it is not the Jew, Shylock, who moves painfully away, but the typical figure of the Jew in the middle ages, that pariah of society who cried in vain for justice? His fate is eminently tragic, not because his rights are denied him, but because he, a Jew of the middle ages, has faith in the law — we might say just as if he were a Christian — a faith in the law firm as a rock which nothing can shake, and which the judge himself feeds until the catastrophe breaks upon him like a thunder clap, dispels the illusion and teaches him that he is only the despised medieval Jew to whom justice is done by defrauding him.

right he had already admitted, to cut a pound of flesh from the living body, the right to the shedding of the blood which necessarily accompanied it. Just as well might the judge deny to the person whose right to an easement he acknowledged, the right to leave foot-marks on the land, because this was not expressly stipulated for in the grant. One might almost believe that the tragedy of Shylock was enacted in the earliest days of Rome; for the author of the Twelve Tables held it necessary to remark expressly in relation to the laceration of the debtor (*in partes secare*) by the creditor, that the size of the piece should be left to his free choice. (*Si plus minusve secuerint, sine fraude esto!*)

The picture of Shylock conjures up another before my mind, the no less historical than poetical one of Michel Kohlhaas, which Heinrich von Kleist has described in his novel of that name with all the fascination of truth. Shylock retires from the scene entirely broken down by grief; his strength is gone and he bows without resistance to the decision of the judge. Not so Michel Kohlhaas. After every means to obtain his rights, which have been most grievously violated, has been exhausted; after an act of sinful cabinet-justice has closed the way of redress to him, and Justice herself in all her representatives, even to the highest, has sided with injustice, a feeling of infinite woe overpowers him at the contemplation of the outrage that has been done him and he exclaims: "Better be a dog, if I am to be trampled under foot, than a man"; and he says: "The man who refuses me the protection of the law relegates me to the condition of the savage of the forest, and puts a club in my hand to defend myself with." He snatches

89

the soiled sword out of the hand of such
venal Justice and brandishes it in a manner
that spreads consternation far and wide
through the country, causes the state to shake
to its very foundations and the prince to
tremble on his throne. It is not, however,
the savage feeling of vengeance that animates
him; he does not turn murderer and brigand,
like Karl Moor, who wished "to make the
cry of revolt resound through all nature to
lead into the fight against the race of hyenas,
air, earth and sea," whose wounded feeling
of justice causes him to declare war against
all humanity; but it is a moral idea which
urges him forward, the idea that "it is his
duty to the entire world to consecrate all his
strength to the obtaining of satisfaction and
to the guarding of his fellow-citizens against
similar injustice." To this idea he sacrifices
everything, his family's happiness, the honor
of his name, all his earthly possessions, his
blood, and his life; and he carries on no aim-
less war of extermination, for he directs it
only against the guilty one, and against all

those who make common cause with him.
At last, when the hope of obtaining justice
dawns upon him, he voluntarily lays down
his arms; but, as if chosen to illustrate by
example to what depth of ignominy the disregard of law and dishonor could descend at
that time, the safe conduct given him, and
the amnesty are violated, and he ends his life
on the place of execution. However, before
his life is taken from him, justice is done
him, and the thought that he has not fought
in vain, that he has restored respect for the
law and preserved his dignity as a human
being, makes him smile at the horrors of
death; and, reconciled with himself, the world,
and God, he gladly and resolutely follows the
executioner. What reflections does not this
legal drama suggest! Here is an honest and
good man, filled with love for his family, with
a simple, religious disposition, who becomes
an Attila and destroys with fire and sword
the cities in which his enemy has taken refuge.
And how is this transformation effected?
By the very quality which lifts him morally

high above all his enemies who finally triumph over him; by his high esteem for the law, his faith in its sacredness, the energy of his genuine, healthy feeling of legal right. The tragedy of his fate lies in this that his ruin was brought about by the superiority and nobility of his nature, his lofty feeling of legal right, and his heroic devotion to the idea of law, which made him oblivious to all else and ready to sacrifice everything for it, in contact with the miserable world of the time in which the arrogance of the great and the powerful was equaled only by the venality and cowardice of the judges. The crimes which he committed fall much more heavily on the prince, his functionaries and his judges, who forced him out of the way of the law into the way of lawlessness. For no wrong which man has to endure, no matter how grievous, can at all compare, at least in the eyes of ingenuous moral feeling, with that which the authority established by God commits when it itself violates the law. Judicial murder is the deadly sin of the law. The guardian and

sentinel of the law is changed into its murderer; the physician poisons his patient; the
guardian strangles his ward. In ancient
Rome, the corrupt judge was punished with
death. For the justice which has violated
the law there is no accuser as terrible as the
sombre, reproachful form of the criminal
made a criminal by his wounded feeling of
legal right — it is its own bloody shadow.
The victim of corrupt and partial justice is
driven almost violently out of the way of
the law; he becomes the avenger of his own
wrong, the executor of his own rights, and it
not infrequently happens that, overshooting
the mark, he becomes the sworn enemy of
society, a robber and a murderer. If, like
Michel Kohlhaas, his nature be noble and
moral, it may guard him against going so
far astray, but he will become a criminal,
and by suffering the penalty of his crime, a
martyr to his feeling of legal right. It is
said that the blood of martyrs does not flow
in vain, and the saying may have been true
of him. It may be that his warning shadow

sufficed for a long time to make the legal oppression of which he was the victim an impossibility.

In conjuring up this shadow, I have desired to show by a striking example how far the very man whose sentiment of legal right is strongest and most ideal may go astray when the imperfection of legal institutions refuses him satisfaction. Here the struggle for law becomes a struggle against the law. The feeling of legal right, left in the lurch by the power which should protect it, itself abandons the ground of the law and endeavors, by helping itself, to obtain what ignorance, bad will, or impotence refuses it. And it is not only a few very strong and violent characters, in which the national feeling of legal right raises its protest against such a condition of things, but this protest is sometimes repeated by the whole population under certain forms, which, according to their object or to the manner in which the whole people or a definite class look upon them or apply them, may be considered as popular substitutes for, and

94

accessories to, the institutions of the state.
Here belong the secret courts of criminal justice in the middle ages and the feudal law,
which bear weighty evidence to the impotence or the partiality of the criminal courts
of the time and to the weakness of the state
power; in the present, dueling, which is a
palpable proof that the penalties which the
state inflicts on attacks on one's honor are
not sufficient to satisfy the delicate feeling
of honor of certain classes of society. Here
also belong the revenge for bloodshed of
the Corsicans and so-called lynch-law in
the United States. All these show very
plainly that the legal institutions of the
country are not in harmony with the feeling
of the people or of a class. They always
imply a reproach to the state, either that it
makes them necessary or that it endures
them. When the law has prohibited them,
without, however, being able to abolish them,
they may become, for the individual, the
source of a very serious conflict. The Corsi-
can who obeys the law rather than have

recourse to revenge for bloodshed is despised by his own kinsfolk; if he follows what the national feeling seems to demand of him, he perishes by the avenging arm of justice. And thus it is with the duel. The person who declines it when his honor dictates that he should accept it, is disgraced; if he accepts it, he is punished — a situation as painful to the individual as to the judge. In vain do we look for facts analogous to these in the early history of Rome, for the institutions of the state were *then* in perfect harmony with the national feeling of legal right.

CHAPTER V

IMPORTANCE OF THE STRUGGLE FOR LAW TO NATIONAL LIFE

I HAVE now reached the end of my reflections on the struggle of the individual for his legal rights. We have followed him through all his motives, from the lowest of mere calculation up to the ideal one of the assertion of his personality and its moral conditions of existence, until we reached the realization of the idea of justice — that highest point, from which one false step plunges the man whose feeling of violated right has made a criminal into the abyss of lawlessness.

But the interest of this struggle is not confined, by any means, to private life or private law. Rather does it extend far beyond them. A nation is, after all, only the sum of all the individuals who compose it, and the nation

thinks, feels, and acts as the individuals that
make it up think, feel, and act. If the feeling
of legal right of the individuals of the nation
is blunted, cowardly, apathetic; if it finds no
room for a free and vigorous development,
because of the hindrances which unjust laws
and bad institutions put in its way; if it meets
with persecution where it should have met
with support and encouragement; if, in consequence of this, it accustoms itself to endure
injustice and to look upon it as something
which cannot be helped, who will believe that
such a slavish, apathetic and paralyzed feeling of legal right can be aroused all at once to
life and to energetic reaction, when there is
question of a violation of the rights, not of
an individual, but of the whole people; an
attempt on their political freedom, the breach
or overthrow of their constitution, or an
attack from a foreign enemy? How can the
person who has not been used to defending
even his own rights feel the impulse voluntarily to stake his life and property for the
community? How can the man who thinks

nothing of the ideal damage which he suffers in his person and his honor, inasmuch as he abandons his rights, because he loves his ease; who was accustomed, in legal matters, to employ only the measure of material interest, be expected to employ a different measure and to feel differently when there is question of the right and the honor of the nation? Whence could that idealism of feeling suddenly proceed which had thus far never shown itself? No! The battler for constitutional law and the law of nations is none other than the battler for private law; the same qualities which distinguished him struggling for his rights as an individual accompany him in the battle for political liberty and against the external enemy. What is sowed in private law is reaped in public law and the law of nations. In the valleys of private law, in the very humblest relations of life, must be collected, drop by drop, so to speak, the forces, the moral capital, which the state needs to operate on a large scale, and to attain its end. Private law, not public law,

is the real school of the political education
of the people, and if we would know how a
people, in case of need, will defend their
political rights and their place among the
nations, let us examine how the separate
members of the nation assert their own right
in private life. I have already cited the
example of the combative Englishman; and
I can only repeat here what I said above:
In the shilling for which he stubbornly struggles the political development of England
lives. No one will dare to wrest from a
people who, in the very smallest matters,
bravely assert their rights, the highest of
their possessions, and it is, therefore, not
mere chance that the same people of anti-
quity who attained to the greatest political
development within, and displayed the greatest power externally, the Romans, had at the
same time the most fully developed system
of private law. Law is idealism — paradoxical as this may seem — not the idealism of
the fancy, but of character: that is, of the
man who looks upon himself as his own end,

and esteems all else lightly when he is attacked
in his personality. What matters it to him
whence this attack upon his rights proceeds—
whether from an individual, from his own
government, or from a foreign nation? It
is not the person of the aggressor that decides
what resistance he shall oppose to the attack,
but the energy of his feeling of legal right,
the moral force with which he is wont to
assert himself. Hence the principle is ever
true: the political position of a people, both
at home and abroad, is always in keeping
with their moral force; the Celestial Empire
with its bamboo, the rod for its adult children,
and its hundreds of millions of inhabitants,
will never attain, in the eyes of foreign
nations, the respected position of little Swit-
zerland. The natural disposition of the Swiss
in the matter of art and poetry is anything
but ideal. It is sober and practical, like
that of the Romans. But, in the sense in
which I have thus far used the expression
"ideal," in its relation to law, it is just as
applicable to the Swiss as to the Englishman.

This idealism of the healthy feeling of legal right would undermine its own foundation if it confined itself to the defense of its own rights only, without taking any part in the maintenance of law and order. It knows not only that in defending its own legal rights it defends the law, but that in defending the law it defends its own legal rights. In a community in which this feeling, this sense for strict law prevails, we look about in vain for the saddening sights so common elsewhere — the mass of the people, when the authorities prosecute the criminal or the violator of the laws or seek to arrest him, taking his part, and seeing in the state power the natural enemy of the people. Every one knows that the cause of the law is his own cause. Only the criminal here sympathizes with the criminal. The honest man does not. Rather does he lend a willing and helping hand to the police and to the authorities.

It will be scarcely necessary for me to express in words the inference to be drawn from what has been said. It is summed up

in the principle: For the state which desires
to be respected abroad, and to be firm and
unshaken internally, there is no more precious
good which it has to guard and foster than
the national feeling of legal right. The foster-
ing of it is one of the highest and most important duties of political pedagogy. In the
healthy, vigorous feeling of legal right of the
individual, the state possesses the most fruitful source of its own strength, the surest
guaranty, from within and from without, of
its own existence. The feeling of legal right
is the root of the whole tree. If the root be
good for nothing, if it withers in the rocks
and in the sand, all the rest is but an illusion;
the storm comes and plucks it up by the
roots. But the trunk and the top have the
advantage that they are seen, while the roots
are hidden in the ground and veiled from sight.
The disastrous influence which unjust laws
and bad legal institutions exercise on the
moral power of the nation acts under ground,
in those regions which so many amateur states-
men do not consider worthy of their atten-

tion; they are concerned only with the stately top; of the poison which rises to the top from the root they have no idea whatever. But despotism knows where it must strike to fell the tree; it leaves the top untouched at first, but destroys the roots. Every despotism has begun with attacks on private law, with the violation of the legal rights of the individual; when its work is done the tree falls of itself. Hence the necessity, above all, of opposing it here, and the Romans well knew what they were doing when they took advantage of an attempt on female chastity and honor to put an end to the kings and the decemvirate. To destroy the feeling of personal liberty in the peasant by means of taxes and services, to put the citizen under the guardianship of the police, to make the permission to go on a journey dependent on the granting of a passport, and the thought of the author on the approval of the censor, to impose taxes according to one's good will and pleasure — even a Machiavelli could have given no better recipe to extinguish

all manly feeling of personal liberty in a
people, and to insure despotism an unresisted
conquest.   That the same door through which
despotism and arbitrariness enter stands open
for the foreign enemy also, is not considered;
and only when the enemy is actually there,
and it is too late, do the wise come to recognize that the moral power and the feeling of
legal right of a people are the most effectual
rampart which can be raised against external
enemies.   It was at the time that the peasant
and citizen were the subjects of feudal and
absolute arbitrariness that Alsace and Lor-
raine were lost to the German Empire.   How
could those provinces have for the empire
a feeling which they had ceased to have for
themselves?

But it is our own fault if we understand the
teachings of history only after it is too late;
it is not its fault if we do not understand them
in time, for it preaches them, always, in such
a manner that we may understand them and
profit by them.   The power of a people is
synonymous with the strength of their feeling

of legal right. The cultivation of the national feeling of legal right is care for the health and strength of the state. By this cultivation and care, I do not, of course, understand schooling and instruction, but the practical carrying out of all the principles of justice in all the relations of life. It is not, however, sufficient to occupy ourselves only with the external mechanism of the law; it may, indeed, be so organized and directed that the most perfect order may reign, and still that the demand above referred to may be entirely ignored. Personal bondage, the tax for protection paid by the Jew, and so many other principles and institutions of times past, which were in the most flagrant contradiction with a strong, healthy feeling of legal right, and which injured the state itself, perhaps, more than the citizens, peasants, Jews, on whom the burthen of them fell, in the first instance, were also conformable to law and order. The fixedness, clearness, certainty of positive law, the doing away with all those principles at which a healthy feeling of legal

right might take offense in any sphere of
the law, not only of private law, but in the
police power, the administrative, financial,
legislative, the independence of the courts,
the greatest possible perfection of legal procedure — this is a surer way to increase the
power of the state than the greatest possible
increase of the military budget. Every pro-
vision which the people feel to be unjust,
and every institution which they detest, is an
injury to the national feeling of legal right
and to the national strength, a sin against
the idea of law, the burthen of which falls
on the state itself, and for which it has not
infrequently to pay dearly. It may, under
certain circumstances, cost it a province. I
am not, indeed, of the opinion that the state
should avoid these sins from reasons of
expediency simply. Rather do I consider
it the most sacred duty of the state to realize
this idea for its own sake; but this may be
doctrinarian idealism, and I have no word of
blame for the practical politician and states-
man who refuses such a demand with a shrug

of the shoulders. And just on this account
have I exposed the practical side of the question to view, the side which he fully understands; for the idea of law and the interest
of the state go, here, hand in hand. There
is no feeling of legal right, no matter how
healthy it may be, which can, in the long
run, resist the influence of bad laws; it grows
blunted, withers and decays. For the essence
of legal right is, as I have frequently remarked
already, action. What the air is to the flame,
freedom of action is to the feeling of legal
right. Refuse it this freedom, and the feeling dies.

CHAPTER VI

THE ROMAN LAW OF TO-DAY, AND THE STRUGGLE FOR LAW

MIGHT stop here, for my subject is exhausted. The reader, however, will allow me to claim his attention for another question closely related to my subject, the question how far our present law, or to speak more accurately, the Roman law of to-day as it obtains here, on which alone I can venture to express a judgment, comes up to the requirements described in the preceding pages. I do not hesitate to say that it does not, in any way, come up to them. It is far behind the rightful claims of a healthy feeling of legal right, and not because it has not, in many cases, found the true solution, but because its way of looking at things is diametrically opposed to the idealism described above as constituting the essence of the healthy feeling of legal right — I mean that idealism which sees in a violation of law an attack not only on the object, but on the person himself. Our civil law does not give this idealism the least support. The measure with which it measures all violations of legal right, with the exception of an attack on a man's honor, is that of material value. It is nothing but the perfect expression of petty, sober materialism.

But what should the law guarantee to the person whose legal rights have been infringed, in his property, but the litigated object or its value? If this be true, the thief, too, might be allowed to depart, who had restored the object stolen. But, we are told, the thief commits a crime not only against the person whom he has robbed, but also against the laws of the state, against order, against the moral law. And does not the debtor who denies the loan which has been made him, the seller or the lessor who breaks his contract, the agent who abuses the confidence I placed in him to overreach me, do the same?

Is it any satisfaction to my wounded feeling of legal right when, from all these persons, I obtain, after a long struggle, only what belonged to me from the beginning? But, even leaving this desire for satisfaction out of consideration, a desire which I do not hesitate to acknowledge to be entirely justifiable, what a disturbance of the natural equilibrium between the parties! The danger with which a bad issue of the suit threatens them consists for the one in the loss of his property, and for the other in the restitution of what he unjustly retained. In the opposite case, the one has the advantage that he loses nothing, and the other that he has added to his wealth at the expense of his adversary. Is not this to provoke the most shameless of lying, and to put a premium on unfaithfulness? But I have thus, in fact, done no more than characterize our law. I shall have an opportunity later to prove this opinion; but I believe that it will be easier to do this, if, for the sake of contrast, I refer to the attitude which the Roman law assumed towards this question.

I distinguish in this respect three stages of development. The first is that, if I may say so, of the boundless violence of the feeling of legal right, not yet capable of self-control, of the older law; the second is that of the measured strength of the feeling of legal right in the intermediate law; the third is that of the decline of the feeling of legal right at the close of the Empire, and especially in the Justinian law.

I here sum up, in a few words, the result of the researches which I have made and published in another work, on the form under which this question appears to us in the first stage of its development. In this stage, such was the sensitiveness of the feeling of legal right that every violation of or attack on one's personal rights was looked at from the standpoint of subjective injustice and the degree of guilt of the aggressor not taken into consideration; and hence the complainant exacted satisfaction for the injury done, both from the person who was only formally guilty and from the person who was really so. The man who denied a plain debt (*nexum*), or the damage which he had done to the chattel of his opponent, paid, if defeated, double; and·so the person who, in a suit for the ownership of a thing, had as holder of it taken its fruits, was condemned to return double the value, and had, besides, to bear the loss, if defeated, of the sum which he had staked on the suit (*sacramentum*). The plaintiff had to suffer the same penalty when he lost the suit, for he had claimed the property of another; and if he erred ever so little in the valuation of an amount to which he was justly entitled, he forfeited the whole amount.

Of these principles and provisions of the older law much has passed over into the more modern law, but the new independent creations of that law breathe an entirely different spirit. It may be described as the employment and application of the measure of guilt in all cases of the violation of private law. Objective and subjective injustice are strictly distinguished. The former entails simply the

restitution of the object, the second a penalty
in addition to this, sometimes a fine, sometimes
disgrace; and this proportionate infliction of
a penalty is one of the soundest thoughts of
the intermediate Roman law. That a deposi-
tary who had become guilty of the breach of
trust of denying the deposit or refusing to
restore it to the depositor, that the agent or
guardian who had used his position of trust
to promote his own interests, or who had
knowingly neglected his duty, should escape
by merely restoring the thing or by making
good the damage caused, was something to
which the healthy feeling of legal right of
the Romans could not reconcile itself. It
demanded, besides this, the infliction of a
penalty for the wrong done, as a satisfaction
of the wounded feeling of legal right and as a
means of deterring others from similar mis-
deeds. The penalties inflicted were, in the
first place, infamy — in Rome one of the
severest imaginable, for it entailed, besides
the social degradation which it produced,
the loss of all political rights, political death.

It was inflicted in all cases in which the infringement of legal rights was an aggravated breach of faith. Then there were the pecuniary penalties, which were much more extensively employed than they are among ourselves. For the person who, in an unjust cause, instituted a suit, or allowed one to be instituted, there was an entire arsenal of such deterrent means in readiness. They began with fractions ($\frac{1}{10}$, $\frac{1}{5}$, $\frac{1}{3}$, $\frac{1}{4}$) of the litigated object, rose to multiples of its amount, under certain circumstances, where the defiance of the opponent could not be broken in any other way, *ad infinitum*, that is, to the amount which the plaintiff declared under oath to be satisfactory. There were especially two forms of procedure, the prohibitory interdicts of the prætor and the *actiones arbitrariæ*, which were intended to compel the accused to desist without any further disadvantageous consequences, or to expect to be considered a willful violator of the law, and to be treated accordingly. They compelled the accused, when he persisted in his resistance, or in his attack, not to restrict his action to the person of the accuser, but to work against the authorities also; and thus it was no longer only the legal rights of the complainant which were in question, but the law itself in the person of its representatives.

The object of these penalties was the same as that of the penalty in criminal law. It was, on the one hand, a purely practical object, to guard the interests of private life against such violations as did not fall under the head of crimes, and, on the other, a moral object, to afford satisfaction to the wounded feeling of legal right; not of the person directly concerned only, but of all those persons who have known of the case, and to reassert the authority of the law. The money was not the end had in view, but only the means to the end.[1]

[1]There is a very strong proof of what I have just said in the *actiones vindictam spirantes.* They show this ideal point of view very clearly, and that their object was not a sum of money or the restitution of a thing, but reparation for an attack on the feeling of legal right, and on the feeling of personality (*magis vindictæ quam pecuniæ habet rationem*). Hence these actions did not survive to the heirs, they could not be assigned, they could not be begun by the

The manner in which the intermediate Roman law looked at this matter is, in my eyes, something wonderful. It was equally far removed from two extremes, from that of the old law, which placed objective injustice on the same level as subjective injustice, and from that of our present law, which taking an opposite direction has lowered the latter to the level of the former. It gave entire satisfaction to the legitimate claims which could be raised by the justest feeling of legal right, for it was not satisfied with strictly separating the two species of injustice, but it could discern and give expression minutely and intelligently to the form, mode, gravity, and to all the shades of subjective injustice.

In turning now to the last stage of development of the Roman law, as it has been definitely fixed, in the Institutes of Justinian, I cannot resist calling attention to the importance of the law of inheritance, both for the

creditors in case of an assignment for their benefit, they were barred after a relatively short period of time, and hence they had no place where it was shown that the injured person had not felt the injustice done him (*ad animum suum non revocaverit. de injur, 47, 10*).

life of the individual and for that of the
nation. What would the law of this period
be, if it had had to create it by its own efforts?
But, just as many heirs, unable to procure for
themselves the necessaries of life, live on the
wealth accumulated by the testator, an
exhausted and degenerated people subsist,
for a long time, on the intellectual capital
of a previous vigorous age. I do not mean
simply that it enjoys the labor of others
without any trouble to itself. I would,
above all, call attention to the fact that it
is in the nature of the works, creations and
institutions of the past to preserve, for a
certain length of time, and to revivify, the
spirit which gave them birth. They hold in
themselves a store of latent force which is
changed into active force by personal contact with them. In this sense the private
law of the republic in which was reflected
the energetic and vigorous feeling which the
old Roman people had for legal right, served
the empire for a time as a living source. In
the great desert of the later world, it was the

118

only oasis in which fresh water flowed. But despotism is like the simoon's breath, which allows no plant to grow; and private law alone not being able to maintain a spirit which was despised everywhere, was obliged to succumb, although latest of all, to the spirit of the new era. This spirit of the new era presents itself to us under a very strange appearance. We might expect to find in it the marks of despotism, severity, harshness, want of consideration, and yet we find the very opposite — mildness and humanity. But this mildness itself is a despotic mildness, that is, it robs one person of what it gives another — it is the mildness of arbitrariness and caprice, not that of humanity — it is the penalty of cruelty. This is not the place to give all the proofs on which I might base this assertion. It will be sufficient, it seems to me, to call attention to one especially significant trait of that character, one which is rich in historical material — the moderation and consideration shown to the debtor at the expense of the creditor. It may, I think, be laid down as a general maxim that sympathy with the debtor is the sign of a weak epoch. This sympathy styles itself humanity. A vigorous age is concerned first of all with insuring the creditor his rights, even if the debtor goes to the wall in consequence.

To come now to the Roman law of the present time: I almost regret that I have mentioned it, for I see myself compelled to pass judgment on it here, without being able to defend it as I would like. But that judgment itself I do not hesitate to express.

To sum up my thoughts on the subject in a few words, I would say that I find in the aggregate of history, and in all the application, of modern Roman law, a marked preponderance, rendered necessary to a certain extent by circumstances, of simple erudition over all those factors which otherwise determine the formation and development of the law: the national feeling of legal right, practice, and legislation. It is foreign law, written in a foreign language, introduced by the learned who alone can understand it perfectly, and exposed, from the first, to the different and changing influence of two entirely opposite interests, frequently in conflict with each other; the influence, I mean, of science, purely and simply historical, and that of the practical application and development of the law. The practice, on the other hand, has not strength sufficient to dominate completely over the spirit of the matter of the law. It is, therefore, condemned to permanent dependence on, to a permanent wardship of, the theory; and hence it is that particularism prevails in legislation and in the administration of justice over the weak and limited efforts made to reach centralization. Can it be a matter of surprise that a gaping abyss stood between such law and the national feeling of legal right, that the people did not understand their law, nor the law the people? Institutions and principles which in Rome were, considering the circumstances and customs of the time there, intelligible, became here, on account of the complete disappearance of their conditions pre-

cedent, a real curse; and there never was in
this world a mode of administering justice
with more power than this to shake a people's
confidence in the law and all belief in its
existence. What can the simple and honest
ordinary man think when the judge, before
whom he appears with a document showing
that his opponent acknowledges an indebtedness to him of a hundred dollars, holds the
signer not to be bound because the document
is a *cautio indiscreta*, or when a document
which expressly mentions a loan as the basis
of an indebtedness is held to have no force as
evidence except after the expiration of two
years?

But I do not intend to enter into details;
there is no telling where this might lead me.
Rather would I confine myself to pointing
out two instances of aberration — I cannot
call them by any other name — in our jurisprudence, which are of a fundamental nature
and which contain the real germs of injustice.

The first consists in this, that our modern
jurisprudence has entirely lost sight of the

simple idea already brought out, that there is question in an infringement of one's legal rights, not merely of a pecuniary value, but of the satisfaction of the wounded feeling of legal right. Its measure is the basest and emptiest materialism — money and nothing else. I recollect having heard of a judge who, when the amount of the object in litigation was small, in order to be relieved of the burthen of the trial, offered to pay the plaintiff out of his own pocket, and who was greatly offended because the offer was refused. That the plaintiff was concerned about the vindication of his legal rights and not about the money, this learned judge could not get through his head; and we cannot blame him for it. He might very easily shift the blame on the science of the law. The money *condemnation* which, in the hands of the Roman magistrate, was one of the most powerful means of doing justice to the ideal feeling of legal right which had been wounded, has become, under the influence of our theory of evidence, one of the sorriest expedients which judicial authority has ever made use of to prevent injustice. The plaintiff is required to prove to a farthing the money-value which he has at stake in the suit. What becomes of the protection of the law where there is no such pecuniary interest? A lessor excludes a lessee from a garden which the latter had contracted to enjoy together with the former. How can the lessee prove the money-value of a sojourn of a few hours in a garden? Or the former lets the dwelling before the lessee has taken actual possession of it to another, and the lessee is compelled to put up with the most miserable accommodation for six months, until he finds another dwelling. An inn-keeper shows a guest to the door to whom he had promised a room by telegraph, and the latter may wander about for hours in the night, in search of the most wretched quarters. Try to estimate this in money, or rather, see what compensation the court will mete out for it. In France, thousands of francs; in Germany nothing at all; for the German judge will reply that inconvenience, no matter

how great, cannot be estimated in money.
A private teacher who has made an engage-
ment with a private institute, subsequently
finds a more agreeable situation, and breaks
his contract; another cannot be had immedi-
ately to take his place. Let any one calculate
the money value lost by the want of instruction of the pupils in French or drawing, for
weeks or months, or the damage in money
sustained by the principal of the institute.
Suppose that a female cook leaves her place
without cause, and that, in consequence, her
master is subjected to the greatest embarrassment, because he finds it impossible to fill it.
How can this embarrassment be estimated in
money? In all these cases, people are in
Germany entirely helpless, for the assistance
which the law offers to one whose legal rights
have been invaded supposes proof which he
never is able to adduce; an assistance which,
even where by way of exception it is possible
to adduce this proof, is not sufficient effectually to oppose injustice from the other side.
This is nothing else but the reign of injustice.

It is not the inconvenience to which one is thus subjected that is most burthensome and wounding in all this; it is the bitter feeling that one's unquestionable rights can be trampled under foot, and that there is no help for it.

We should not hold the Roman law responsible for these defects; for although it has always held to the principle that final judgment should always have a money basis, it always knew how to apply the money *condemnation* in such a manner that it effectually protected not only pecuniary interests, but all other rightful interests. The *condemnation* to pay a sum of money was the means of pressure which the judge employed in civil matters to insure obedience to his orders. The defendant who refused to do what the judge imposed on him to do, did not get off with the mere money value of the obligation he owed, but the money *condemnation* here performed the functions of a penalty, and this consequence of the suit assured the plaintiff a satisfaction to which, under some circum-

126

stances, he attached much more importance than to the money; viz., the moral satisfaction for the frivolous violation of his legal rights. Our present law never affords this satisfaction; it knows nothing of it; it takes cognizance only of the money-value of the obligation which has not been met.

In keeping with this insensibility of our present law for the ideal interest affected by a violation of legal right is the doing away with, in modern practice, of the penalties inflicted by private Roman law. The faithless bailee no longer incurs infamy among us. The greatest piece of rascality, if its perpetrator is only skillful enough to evade the criminal law, escapes in our day, entirely free and unpunished. On the other hand, money-penalties (*Geldstrafen*) and the penalties of *frivolous denial*, figure in the law books, but they are never applied in practice. But what does this mean? Only that with us subjective injustice is reduced to the level of objective injustice. Between the debtor who shamelessly denies the loan made him and

the heir who does the same thing in good
faith; between the agent who has deceived
me and the one who has simply made a mis-
take, our present law knows no difference.
Everywhere the trial turns only on the bare
money interest. Our lawyers to-day are so
far from believing that the balance of Justice
should, in private law as well as in criminal
law, weigh the injustice which has been done,
and not only the pecuniary interest, that, in
daring to speak about it, I must expect to
hear it objected that in this precisely lies
the difference between criminal law and the
law pertaining to the rights of persons. Yes,
this is true of our actual law, unfortunately
true, but it is not true of law in itself. It
would be first necessary to prove to me
that there is one part of the law in which the
idea of justice should not be realized to its
full extent. But the idea of justice is insep-
arable from the carrying out of the idea of
culpability.

The second instance of aberration of our
modern jurisprudence, referred to above, con-

sists in the theory of evidence which it establishes. One might think that theory had been invented only for the purpose of frustrating the law. If all the debtors in the world had conspired together to deprive creditors of their rights, they could have devised no more effectual means to reach that end than has our jurisprudence by means of this theory of evidence. No mathematician can set up a more exact method of proof than the one which our jurisprudence employs. It reaches the acme of irrationality in the actions for damages. The mischief, to employ the language of a Roman jurist,[1] "caused here to the law under the appearance of law," and the beneficent contrast which the intelligent mode of action of the French tribunals offers, have been described in so many recent works that I need not add anything on it; one thing alone I cannot refrain from saying: Woe to the plaintiff, well for the defendant!

[1] *Paulus* in l. 91, p. 3, de V. O. (45, 1) "*in quo genere plerumque sub autoritate juris scientiæ perniciose erratur.*" Only the jurist had here another aberration in view.

If I were to sum all that I have thus far said, I might call this last exclamation the watchword of our modern jurisprudence and practice. It has advanced far on the road on which Justinian entered; it is not the creditor, but the debtor, who awakens its sympathy, and it would rather sacrifice the rights of a hundred creditors than, by any possibility, deal too severely with a debtor.

The person not versed in the law might almost believe that it was scarcely possible to add anything to this partial lawlessness, the legacy to us of a false theory of legists, who busy themselves with our civil law and mode of procedure; and yet, even this theory is surpassed by the aberration of former criminalists, which may be characterized as an attempt on the very idea of law and as the most odious crime against the feeling of legal right committed by science. I here refer to the shameful paralyzing of the right of self-defense, that original right of man, which, as Cicero says, is a law enacted by nature itself, and which the Roman jurists were ingenuous enough to believe could not be ignored in any body of laws in the world. ("*Vim vi repellere omnes leges omniaque jura permittunt.*") They might have been convinced of the contrary in the last century, and even in our own. The learned gentlemen, indeed, admitted this right in principle, but feeling for the criminal the same sympathy felt by the jurists of the civil law and its mode of procedure for the debtor, they endeavored in practice to limit and curtail it, in such a manner that they protected the guilty and left the person attacked unprotected. What a deep abyss of the degeneration of the feeling of personality, of unmanliness, of the decay and bluntness of the sentiment of legal right opens before us, when we descend into the literature of this theory! We might almost imagine ourselves in the company of a set of chaste, emasculated men. The man whose life or honor is threatened, we are told, should retire or take flight — that is, yield the field to injustice — and these sages disagreed only on one question: whether officers, nobles and other persons of position should flee also. A poor soldier who, to obey this order, had retreated twice, but who, being pursued by his adversary, finally resisted and killed his pursuer, was condemned to death as a salutary lesson to himself and as a deterrent example to others.

People of very high position and of distinguished birth, likewise officers, should be permitted to make rightful resistance in defense of their honor; but, adds another, in limitation of this, in case of mere verbal injury, they should not go as far as killing. There were, on the other hand, other persons, even state officials, who could not be allowed to enjoy this privilege; and the ministers of civil justice were dismissed with the remark that "as mere men of the law, spite of all their claims, they had to depend on the law of the land and the rights it accorded to all alike, and that they could make no further pretensions." The merchant class fared worst of all. "Merchants, even the richest," we read, "constitute no exception. Their honor

is their credit; they have honor only so long
as they have money; they may, therefore,
without any danger of losing their honor or
reputation, bear being called opprobrious
names, and when they belong to the lower
class, put up with a slap, if not very painful,
or a rap over the nose." If the unfortunate
man was a Jew or peasant, he was, for violat-
ing this prescription, to bear the penalty of
prohibited self-defense, whereas other persons
were to be punished as "gently as possible."

But what is especially edifying is the manner in which it was attempted to exclude the
right of self-defense when a question of property was involved. The law of property,
some said, was just like that of honor, a
reparable loss; the former was repaired by the
reivindicatio, the latter by the *actio injuri-
arum*. But how if the robber has taken to his
heels and escaped to foreign parts, and no one
knows who or where he is? The owner has
still *de jure* the *reivindicatio*, and "it is only
the consequence of accidental circumstances,
entirely independent of the nature of the

right of property, that, in some cases, the complaint does not always lead to the proposed end." With this the person may console himself who carries everything he owns upon his person in the form of valuable papers. He still holds his property and the *reivindicatio*, and the robber has nothing but *actual* possession! This reminds me of the man who, when robbed, consoled himself with the reflection that the robber had not the directions for the use of the stolen object. Others admit that, when the loss of a very large sum is involved, it is allowable to employ force, only as a last resort, but they make it the duty of the person attacked, no matter under how great excitement he may be laboring, carefully to consider how much force is required to repel the attack. If he needlessly cracks the skull of the aggressor, where any one who had previously had an opportunity to subject the strength of the skull to an exact examination would have been able to render him harmless by a less powerful stroke, he is held responsible! On the other hand, in the case of less valuable objects, for instance, a gold watch or a purse with a few guldens, or even with a hundred guldens, he must not, for the life of him, do any harm to his aggressor. For what is a watch in comparison with life and limb? The loss of the former can be repaired; the loss of the latter is irreparable. This is an indisputable truth, but that the watch belongs to the person attacked and the limbs to the robber, is forgotten. Doubtless they have for him an incalculable value, for the person attacked they have none at all; and then remains the question: Who repairs the loss of the watch?

But enough of this learned folly and perversity. How deeply humbled we should feel at seeing that the thought, so simple, just, and so much in harmony with the true feeling of legal right, that, in every legal right, be its object only a watch, one's person and all his rights are attacked, had vanished from the law to such an extent that the sacrifice of one's rights and the cowardly flight from injustice could be raised to the dignity of a duty. Can we wonder that cowardice and the apathetic endurance of injustice were the character of our national history at a time when science dared to enunciate such doctrines? Let us congratulate ourselves that we live in very different times. Such theories are impossible in our days. They can thrive only in the swamp through which a nation, rotten alike from a political point of view and from the point of view of law, drags itself along.

This theory of cowardice, of the obligation of sacrificing our imperiled rights, is the most direct opposite of the theory which I have advocated, that the courageous battle for one's legal rights is a strict duty. Not quite so far, yet far enough below the height of this healthy feeling of legal right, lies the level of the view of a modern philosopher, Herbart, as to the ultimate basis of the law. Herbart sees the basis of all law in an æsthetic motive — we can call it nothing else; the dislike of contention. This is not the place to show the complete untenableness of this view, and I am happy to be able to refer to the

writings of Julius Glaser for a refutation of
it. But if we were warranted to estimate
the law from an æsthetic point of view, I do
not know whether, instead of seeing what is
beautiful in the law in the exclusion of a
struggle, I would not rather place it in the
admission of a struggle. I have the courage
to express an opinion in direct opposition to
Herbart's, and frankly to confess myself
guilty of finding pleasure in strife. I of course
do not here mean a mere war of words, or a
contest about nothing. I mean that sublime
struggle in which the man stakes his own
person and all he has for his own rights or
the rights of his country. The person who
blames the love of struggle in this sense may
wipe out all our literature and all our art from
the Iliad of Homer and the sculpture of the
Greeks to our own day. There is scarcely
any subject which has had so much attraction for the pen of the poet and the brush of
the painter as strife and war; and we would
have to go far to find the person whose æsthetic taste is more displeased than pleased

at the contemplation of the higher display of
human power which sculpture and poetry
have illustrated. The highest problem of
art and literature is man's defense of an idea,
be that idea law, fatherland, faith, or truth.
But this entering the lists for an idea is always
a struggle.

It is not, however, æsthetics, but ethics,
which has to tell us what is in harmony with,
and what contradicts, the idea of law. But
ethics, far from rejecting the struggle for
law, enjoins it as a duty. The element of
strife and of struggle which Herbart would
eliminate from the idea of the law is an inte-
gral part of it, and has been from the first—
struggle is the eternal labor of the law. The
sentence: "In the sweat of thy brow shalt
thou eat bread," is on a level with this other:
"By struggling shalt thou obtain thy rights."
From the moment that the law gives up its
readiness to fight, it gives itself up; for the
saying of the poet, that only he deserves liberty and life who has to conquer them for
himself every day, is true of law also.